Rebecca Stepp Revels

Blessed

Blessed

Copyright ©2009 Rebecca Stepp Revels

All rights reserved. No part of this publication may be reproduced, or stored in a database retrieval system, distributed or transmitted, in any form or by any other means, electronic, mechanical, photocopying, recording or otherwise, without the prior written permission of the author.

ISBN 978-0-578-02981-8

Cover photography by Rebecca Stepp Revels

Rebecca Stepp Revels

    I offer this collection of inspirational writes in hopes of glorifying my Lord and Savior.

    The collection included in this book, are words that I feel I have been gifted and blessed with to share with any and all who feel lead to read them. They are words impressed on my heart to put to print. Many is the occasion that I have heard that I have good timing. I have said many times and I will continue to say that the Lord knows what needs to be read, who it is that needs to read it and exactly when it is that the words are needed. It is not my timing but the timing of the Lord above who reaches out to us all in our time of need. All we in turn, need do is be there to accept and receive what it is that He so freely offers.

    I feel blessed and humbled to be used as a vessel in the hands of our Lord and Savior. My hope is that those reading this will find blessings of their own.

Blessed

<u>Blessed</u>

I am blessed Lord in You
I see that every day
in the morning sun, rising
bringing light to a darkened world
there is You, bringing light
to a darkened heart
a heart wounded and weary
that finds rest in You
I am blessed Lord, in You
as I see the crystal blue sky
the greens of the newly budding leaves
the flowers that emerge to dance in the breeze
I see You, even when the eyes are tired
of seeing the pain of this place
in You, in the gifts You give
I see a refuge, a shelter from the storm of this life
I know I am blessed
when I step out into this place
I find You waiting, wishing to walk with me
be with me in love as I find solace here
I hear Your voice, telling me
to be still and hear You
to be still and see You
to be still and know that You are Lord
I know I am blessed
as I feel You move in my heart
calming my storms, easing my fears
taking me to safe harbor in You to rest
when the tears flow freely
from a soul over joyed at Your presence
when the trembling comes as I feel You move
the smile spreads outward and my eyes look upward
to You, with raised hands I praise You
knowing I am so blessed
when I see the compassionate acts of others

Rebecca Stepp Revels

reaching out, as You inspire
when I hear a child sing and laugh
feel the touch of the aged, trembling and gentle
when I stand under the boughs of a tree and watch a soft rain falling down
I know I am in the shelter of Your love
I know, Lord, I know
I am blessed.

~~~~~~~~~~~~~~~~

In You, My Sweet Lord

You Lord
are my place of rest
I seek You, come to You
when life in itself, beats me down
I come to You, when the troubles come
causing me worry, knowing Lord,
that we were not given a spirit of fear
so I seek You, kneeling at the foot of the cross
hand over my worries to You
You Lord
are my sustenance
when my soul hungers and my spirit thirsts
I seek You, I listen for Your voice
Your word is my bread,
Your promises quench my thirst
I know, that You are my Lord
my Savior and Salvation
I know, that eternity with You waits for me
You Lord
are my peace
when the storms come
when the temptations and battles of this life grow
surrounding me, trying to bring me into strife
I seek You, and You are my refuge

Blessed

You bring me to a place of security
where still waters calm the soul of its troubles
in You Lord, I am blessed
In You Lord, I am forgiven
In You Lord, I am redeemed
You Lord,
my sweet Lord
I am loved.

When the Loneliness Comes

and then without warning
the loneliness comes
out of nowhere, from everywhere
wrapping itself around me
like an unseen spider's web
strangling my heart
leaving me empty, aching
hurting
reaching out for that missing touch
seeking, a resolution to the emptiness
You see me Lord, walking in my pain
and You comfort me
showing me, that no matter what comes
You are here, walking with me always
bringing me a peace of heart
a calming of the soul
rest when I am troubled and weary
Walking with You Lord
I find all I need
for You are here to show me
that no matter what comes
You are here with me
You are in control
and all is well.

Rebecca Stepp Revels

<u>You Understand</u>

Tears fill my eyes
as falling to my knees
I come to You Lord
for I know, You understand
this world is a difficult place
the pain that it can inflict
words hard as nails
driven into the heart
words, sharp as barbs
slice into the soul
how You understand
as You hear my cries
see my tears
hanging here, on this suffering
stretched to the limit in my pain
falling to my knees
I see the shadow
I see the cross
and I know, You understand
the suffering and the pain
this place can inflict
You dear Lord
bore the pain,
of the nails piercing Your hands and feet
felt the barbs of the whip, of the twisted thorns
as they tore Your flesh
stretched to the limit and left to die
willingly paying the price
for so great is Your love
falling to my knees
I tremble as I hear Your voice
feel Your presence so very close
assuring me once again
You understand.

Blessed

<u>It Would Be</u>

In You Lord
only in You
do I find the peace I seek.

In You Lord
do I find
the beauty of this place
a gift given to us
by You.
Created out of nothing
spoken into being.
Things that You had no need of
but were created, for us.

I look about me
in the clutter of this life
it would be all too easy, to lose You
allow the things that make me busy
to cover You, hide Your voice
making You difficult to hear
but I ask Lord,
help me always to look to this gift
to see You, in all things
great and small
to always feel You
above all else
close to me.
It would be
all too easy Lord
to allow the storms that come
to have me running to hide
cowering in fear

Rebecca Stepp Revels

as the winds, cover Your voice
making it difficult to hear
my fear in the darkness,
hiding Your light
help me dear Lord
to stand upon You, a rock in shifting sands
a rock in the winds
allowing me, helping me
to hear Your voice, speaking to me
calming the storm,helping me, to feel Your presence
always close, always here.
It would Lord
it would
be all too easy to slip and to fall

help me dear Lord
to look around me, to see what You have created
given to me, blessed me beyond measure
help me Lord,
to hear Your voice, to feel Your presence
to know, always know
Your love.

Blessed

<u>I Am Here</u>

Tenderly You call
hear me

Your voice a whisper in the wind
the laughter of a child
the wisdom of the aged
the song, of a bird, high above

Gently You call
feel my presence

in the love of a friend
in the touch of compassion
a movement, deep in your heart

Sweetly You call
know me

hear My voice
speaking to you
reminding you that in all things
I am here
walking with you always
if you would only see
reminding you, that at all times
I am here
seeing you when you cry
when you laugh at the silly things
I am here, when you call to me
when the darkness of the storms threaten
when the skies are their most brilliant blue
I am here
walk with me

Rebecca Stepp Revels

<u>In The Dust</u>

In my heart
I walk the dusty road of Jerusalem
following Lord, in Your footsteps
listening to Your words as You teach
seeing Your power as You reach out
and with only a touch, heal the sick and lame
I am amazed Lord, at what I see in You
Your gentle and compassionate touch
as You reach out to all, the young, and the elderly
You call Lord, to the rich and the poor
the faithful and the sinner
calling them all Lord, to You
telling one and all of the Father's Kingdom
teaching one and all, of the Father's love
compassionate above all others
Your love shines forth, in Your very walk
drawing the masses to You, where ever You are
I watched You Lord, take such a small amount
and feed the thousands
calm the storms, with no more than a word
I heard, as You blessed the children
explaining how to enter the Father's Kingdom
one must be as a child.
In my heart I wondered of these things
as I walked, those dusty roads
following, in Your footsteps
placing my feet, in the prints Your sandals made in the sand
trembling, I reach out, hoping to merely touch the edge of Your robe
trembling as You turn, and Your gaze falls upon me
with the gentlest of smiles, You reach out and place Your hand on my cheek
as I fall to my knees before You
hearing Your words, that my faith, has set me free
tears flow freely, unchecked from my eyes
streaking my dust covered cheeks,
as the greatest of love, fills and overflows from my heart

Blessed

joy before this unknown fills my soul
there on that dusty road in Jerusalem
in my heart, I see it all
in my heart, I feel Your presence, here on this busy street
walking among the many, yet feeling apart
I feel You, standing here, in this place with me

where I once was so alone
filling me, with Your presence
I see You, in the hands of others, reaching out with compassion
to the very young, and the very old
offering a helping hand, to one in need
feeding the hungry, giving water to the thirsty
a place of rest, for those that have nowhere to go
I see You Lord, in those that do Your work
in those, that follow Your commands
I hear Your words, in the work place, and in Your House
in the dust of this life, I fall to my knees reaching out
hoping to touch, the hem of Your robe
to see You look down to me, and smile
offering Your hand, as You speak,
Your words, telling me
well done, your faith, has set you free.
so that this heart, in this time, in this place
will be filled to overflowing, with Your love
filled, with Your forgiveness and Your peace
and I will walk in Your footsteps
placing my feet, in Your prints in the dust.

~~~~~~~~~~~~~~~~~~~~

Rebecca Stepp Revels

Forgive Me Lord

Forgive me when my words are harsh
spoken, out of an unacceptable emotion
slipping out from an unguarded tongue
sharp and swift, they cut like a two edged sword
doing harm, causing pain, to those that hear
forgive me, when I speak an untruth
whether it is by accident, unknowingly done
or spoken in a way to make a hard fact, easier to take
forgive an untruth spoken for any reason, for there is no excuse
forgive me, when I gossip
the tongue a viper, causing pain to those spoken of
for if when we speak of others, and it doesn't build them up
it tears them down, and that Lord, is not what You asked us to do
forgive me, should my words, be judgmental
You have told me, that is not my place
let me not speak in a way, detrimental to any one, for any thing
forgive me, when words I say, are contrary to Your will.
for I know, they poison the heart
they bring harm, to those that hear, and suffer from them
forgive me, when my words, are not Your words
words that You, would have me to say, in the day to day
Lord,
give those that I have spoken wrongly to
the ability, the grace, to forgive me
as You forgive me

Forgive me Lord, when I fail You in my actions
when I know, what it is that You would have me do
and I turn away, afraid
forgive me, when I know where You would have me go
and instead, I hide away, make excuses, and do not go
forgive me Lord
when I fail You, due to the frailties of this human form

Blessed

give me the strength Lord, to recognize better Your instructions
to hear Your voice and to follow Your will
Help me Lord, to ever walk in Your footsteps
speaking the words, You would have me say
doing the things, that You would have me do
without asking why, without offering excuse
help me Lord, to have the wisdom and strength
to just do.

Help me Lord, to recognize You, in all things
hear Your voice, in all things
and follow Your will, in all things

knowing yet, that when I slip and fall
trip and stumble in this walk, I know
in my heart and in my soul that You Lord will
forgive me.

~~~~~~~~~~~~~~~~~~~~~

Gifts

Treasures waiting
special gifts
found along the way
placed there
to bring a smile
joy to the heart
in the beauty they bring
simple things
delicate and gentle
fill the place with peace
and the eye
with joy.

Rebecca Stepp Revels

<u>For Those That Have Been Given Much</u>

Lord
as I stand among the many blessings
that You have given to me
Help me Lord to remember
those in need
for as You have said
those that have been given much
much will be expected*
and dear Lord
You have indeed given much to me
in the way of Your love
the peace that settles in my heart
and lets me know all is well
the knowledge and understanding
that You grace me with
so that I do not travel this journey in confusion
the knowledge and understanding
of Your Word, so that I may share You
with others that may not know You
share with others the blessings You give
Your presence in my life
giving to my heart a joyous song to sing
and my spirit cause to dance
along this journey Lord
You have given me a close family
and many good friends
that help to encourage, teach and strengthen me
as I walk along this way.
for all this Lord
I thank you
I ask Lord
that will all these things
I am never slow to do as You would have me

Blessed

to reach out a comforting hand
to share warmth, food or a safe place
to understand, that Your love is for all
the clean and the dirty
the wealthy and the poor
the well fed and the hungry
especially Lord those that hunger for You
help me Lord, to remember

and use the blessings You've given me
to bless others.
for I know, to those that have been given much
much will be expected.*
* Paraphrased Luke 12: 48

Rebecca Stepp Revels

<u>Alone No More</u>

In the quiet of the night
when the world is at rest
all is silent, all is calm
I hear You
Whispering to me
drawing me closer to You
telling me, all is well
In the silence of the night
when I feel alone,
an outsider, looking in
trembling in the cold
I feel You
wrapping me in Your love
telling me, all is well
In the silence of the night
when things of the dark bear down
haunting my heart
tormenting my soul
reminding me of things I have done
I hear You
speaking to me
I feel You
wrapping me in Your forgiveness
Then I know, sweet Lord how I know
Your mercy and Your grace
and in the darkest of nights
I feel alone, no more.

Blessed

<u>Restore Me</u>

Feeling Your presence
flowing over me filling my heart
knowing You are here with me
always
knowing, that when I stumble
when I fall
You, Lord, are there to catch me
lift me up, restore me
to the beauty that I find
walking with You
restore me
to the peace You offer
the love You freely
and so abundantly give
When this earthly body is weary
the spirit within grows weak
You are here, always here
with a word, You give me strength
restore me
to the power of Your mercy
the abundance, of Your grace
restore me
to the joy
that I find always there
walking with You.

Rebecca Stepp Revels

<u>You Will</u>

I know Lord
that you hear me
when I cry.

When things get too hard
pressures and temptations
reach out, calling to me
when worries of this life
overwhelm me
threaten to drown me
You see me
when I fall to my knees
nearing breaking under the pressure
tears spilling over
trailing down already tracked cheeks
trembling under the burden
that weighs heavily, too heavily
on a breaking heart
I know, how I know
that You see my tears
You see my struggles
as I try to remain strong
even as the weariness comes
and this body in its earthly frailty stumbles
fearing the darkness that comes
while I seek Your light
need Your guidance
You see my struggles
You hear my cries
and You reach out to me.
In Your healing touch I find mercy
I find the peace, that I can find no where else
a calming that can come
only from You
strength to continue on

Blessed

rest, that brings a peaceful healing
You hear my cries
and You reach out
and dry my tears
lift me out of my fears
protecting me, from the temptations I fight

You hear my cries
and You touch my heart
reminding me once again
that You are with me

will never leave me
will always guide me
will always
love me.

~~~~~~~~~~~~~~~~

I am Thankful that I Did Not Turn Away

I'm so very thankful
that I didn't walk away
that day
when I heard Your voice
speaking in my heart
calling me
I'm so very thankful
that I didn't turn away
ignoring Your voice
making a choice
remaining in darkness
apart from You
I'm so very thankful

Rebecca Stepp Revels

that I didn't close my ears
to Your voice in my heart
whispering truths
I needed to hear
whispering Your word
that I needed to know
I'm so very thankful
that I didn't turn away
that day
when You spoke to me
calling me to You
I'm so very thankful
that I didn't refuse the gift
the blessing You offered
through great mercy and love
the gift of life eternal
the gift of a loving Savior
the gift of forgiveness
I'm so very thankful
that I didn't turn away.

Blessed

You Were There, Waiting

Once broken and lost
wandering alone and afraid
a voice spoke in my heart
one I had walked away from so long ago
calling to me,
seeking me
having never turned away from me
allowing me to take the path of my choosing
but never leaving me alone there
Knowing that this path would be hard
I stumbled and fell
the rocks of this path tearing fragile skin
leaving me bruised and torn
weeping I struggled up and stumbled forward
only to fall, time and again
finally at a place so low
a place so dark the light could not break through
as tears of regret, despair, loss fell
I heard Your voice, calling
I felt Your presence once again so near
I turned to You, the sound of Your calling
reaching out to You
knowing in my heart, that only You could save me
from a hell of my own making
clutching You to my heart, You lead me away
back to Your light and love
back to a place of beauty
resting in You I healed
resting in You, I found Your forgiveness and love
realizing, that even as I walked that wrong path
I had never lost them
as You were never far away
merely waiting on me to realize and turn around
for You were there, waiting.

Rebecca Stepp Revels

Once broken and lost
now healed
and safe in the arms and love
of You, my Savior, my Lord

<u>Singing Praises</u>

I glorify Your name Lord
I sing praises to You
for it is You, and You alone
that have brought me this far

I sing praises to Your name Lord
for You have brought me through the storms
bringing me to safe harbor
giving peace to my heart.

I sing praises to Your name Lord
showing me Your merciful grace,
when none is deserved
in this You that has taught me love

I sing praises to Your name Lord
for You have walked with me
being my Light in the darkest of times
my Salvation and my Hope.

I sing praises to Your name Lord
Your forgiveness is my peace
Your love is my joy
Your Word, is food for my soul.

I sing praises to Your name Lord
my voice rings out in jubilant song
I raise my hands to You Lord, as I fall to bended knee
singing praises to Your name Lord, singing praises to Your name.

Blessed

<u>To Walk In Your Light</u>

To walk in Your light Lord
is all I ask
to hear Your voice speaking to me
whispering encouragement
shouting Your love
to feel Your magnificent peace
wrapped around me securely
comforting me in all things
letting me know You are near
to know Your word
keep it securely in my heart
so that at any given time
they will come to me, comforting
allowing me to know You
to walk in Your light Lord
to hear Your voice
to feel Your presence
telling me, reminding me constantly
You are here, with me
always
as I walk in Your light

Rebecca Stepp Revels

<u>In You Lord, Lies My Strength</u>

When I am weary Lord
this body tired and worn
when just walking is a struggle
I look to You, and find rest

When the worries of this life
like a great storm surround me
the winds of concern blow hard
I look to You, and find a port in the storm

When every day struggles
become too much to bear
and I fight under the heavy load
I look to You, and You lift my burdens

When doubts and fears cause me to feel lost
and so very afraid
when the darkness threatens to over come
I look to You, and You are my Light

When this life becomes difficult
each day a fight to survive
each step sluggish and slow
I look to You, for You Lord, are my salvation

In You, when all goes wrong
I find my peace, I find my comfort
in You, when my soul hungers, I find You are the bread of Life
for You Lord, are my all, my strength, in You, I can go on.

Blessed

<u>How Can I Not Sing Praises</u>

How Lord, can I not sing praises to Your name
when things of the day bring problems
I turn my Lord to You
when worries and fears surround me
as a dark cloud attempting to hide the light
I turn Lord, and give them to You
giving all to You and I have peace
for I know Your love, I know Your comfort
You are my salvation and my Rock
offering me everything in an eternity with You
You take care of my needs Lord
whether they be of material or emotional things
How Lord, can I not, sing praises to Your name?
when You walk with me, through each trial
guiding me always toward You
with the Light that is Your love.
with the peace, that is Your forgiveness
Your presence, comforting me always.

Rebecca Stepp Revels

<u>As You Would</u>

Dear Lord I come to You in humble supplication
asking Lord, in quiet voice
let my thoughts be pure
let no anger dwell there, for it grows as a cancer
spreading, waiting for a moment of inattention
to escape and do harm
for all it takes is a moment
so I ask Lord, for Your peace
I ask Lord, for Your patience
the ability to ignore injustices, as their moment of pain is brief
I come to You Lord, asking in quiet voice
let my heart be true
innocent and just, compassionate to the needs of those I see
whether it be a hand up, or a simple word given of kindness
let my heart have the strength, to act when needed
taking care of those around me, as You my Lord would do
In all things Lord, I simply ask, let me be, like You
walking in Your footsteps, my thoughts always centered on You
seeing this life, as You would
touching those around me, even if unrealized
as You would Lord
let me leave this place, having left something good
a smiling moment of loving peace
a tender moment of compassion
a time however brief, of joy
as You would Lord, as You would.

Blessed

<u>A Voice Crying Out In The Wilderness of This Time</u>

A voice crying out, in the wilderness of this time
please Lord, let me be
place in my heart the words to speak
truths that You would have me to say
telling those that will hear
about You my Lord, all about You
give to me the words of peace
of how you are with us through all storms
teach me Lord, Your words of comfort
for when life's worries strike hard
give me Lord, Your words of forgiveness
of Your awesome mercy and grace
and the strength Lord, and the wisdom
to share those words
with all Lord, that will hear.
Let me be Lord, a voice crying out
in the wilderness of this time
so that those that are lost Lord without You
those that do not know You
can gain understanding and knowledge
that they Lord, can find their way to You
that those that hear Lord,
will open their hearts, their lives, to You Lord.
Let me be, a voice in the wilderness of this time
crying out, for You.

Rebecca Stepp Revels

<u>For You</u>

Remember through all of time
every time, that you do this
remember
for my body was broken
damaged and torn, for you
my blood, I freely shed
for you.

I came to this place for a reason
born of a virgin, born of lowly birth
leaving my Father's side
in Heaven on high
for You

Years I spent. living and learning
growing into a man
when the day came
and my ministry on earth, began
for you

What I wanted for all to hear
with their ears, and held in their heart
was of the love and forgiveness of the Father
the compassion, His mercy and grace
for you

all I ask is acknowledgment
of the transgressions that have been done
all I ask is acceptance, that in your heart you know
that I am indeed the Son
come, for You

I went to the cross freely
knowing that this must come to be

Blessed

it was the only way to life
the only way, you could be set free
I did this, for you

remember

but it did not end
with a death of the cross
burial in a tomb
three days only to wait. before
I lived again, for you

Acceptance is what I ask
believe in who I am
confess your belief
confess your sin
accept these things I have done for you in love
accept the forgiveness I have
for you

~~~~~~~~~~~~~~~~~~~~~~~~~~~~

<u>While Waiting For Sleep to Come</u>

Trembling in the night, waiting for sleep to come
listening to the night sounds around me
as I slip further down under the cover
chilled, but finding warmth beginning
yet I think Lord, of those outside
those with no real place to lay their head
no blankets, no pillows
and my heart breaks for them

Rebecca Stepp Revels

out there, somewhere
trembling in the night, waiting for sleep to come

In the night, my belly rumbles, that last meal hours ago
but I know, that come morning a full cupboard waits
and I will have a way to stop the complaining
yet, I think Lord, of those outside
whose cupboard, is a dumpster behind a cafe
whose breakfast, is a discarded scrap of food
or there is nothing at all
with nothing stored, nothing hidden away
and their belly complains on, as their hunger grows.

I awake, to a warm home and coffee brewing in the pot
struggling to awaken fully and start my day
I speak with You Lord, thanking You, for these blessings
as I go about my preparations, mechanically
but then my heart wanders, to those outside
trembling in the cold, with no where to go
no need to rise early, or at all
and they struggle, just to survive
do they speak to You, do they know You
do they have, the hope of You and an eternity of peace and rest
or do they wander, lost in this world.

help me Lord, give to me a way
to serve You, by being of service to these
the least among us, yet still Your children
help me Lord, that on the nights that I tremble
waiting for sleep, I know that in some way
I have touched those that have no earthly home

giving them a chance to see You
to know You, and plant a seed for You
help me Lord, to find a way
that they too, may be warm,

Blessed

that they too, may be fed
and that they too, may have You to speak with
when they lay, trembling,
waiting for sleep to come.

~~~~~~~~~~~~~~~~~~~~~~~~~

I am Unashamed

I love You Lord
of my faith in You, I am not ashamed
for You are my strength
when I am weak
You know when I hunger
and You feed my soul
You are the Bread of Life
Your word, a blessing
when my spirit thirsts
You are the Living Water
reviving me, refilling me
refreshing me
to go forward again
stronger, ready to share Your light for You are the Light,
come to show the way to a dark world
I love You Lord
of my faith in You, I am unashamed
for You have walked with me faithfully
guiding me as a Shepherd would
through the storms that have come
bringing me to safe harbor
giving to me a place to rest
showing me daily Lord
Your love
giving to me the needs of this body
assuring me of the strength I need

Rebecca Stepp Revels

to do Your will
giving to me, the needs of this life
for You do provide Lord
Your strength, Your peace, Your merciful grace
You do provide Lord
Your forgiveness
but always and forever
Your love

<u>The Peace That is You</u>

Help me dear Lord
to see as You see
the ones around me
that are in need.

those that reach out trembling hands
seeking help, seeking more
yet not knowing what
help me see
not only see,
but reach out in compassion
with a gentle hand.
Offering to them a hand up
a touch on the shoulder
that reaches the heart
offering to them
hope, that there is more
a better place, a better way

help me dear Lord
that I may act
as You would have me
as I seek those in need

Blessed

the ones that are lost
trapped in the darkness of this place
addicted, to the poisons
abusing or being abused
help me Lord
to reach out to them
show them the way
to the Light You offer
the healing love that is You
the peace that You bring to the soul

help me dear Lord
that I may share
with those that I find
lost, alone, in need
Your blessings

for those that are tired
weary of the battle that is fought
just to survive
worn, from the struggle
to make one more day
for those that hunger
thirsting, for more
than what this place has to offer
while they struggle
stumbling their way on
fighting just to survive

help me Lord
that I may offer to them
the knowledge of You
and Your merciful love

for those that are among us
weaker and afraid
to those that are poor

Rebecca Stepp Revels

of spirit, and of health
poor in the ways the world considers important
help me Lord
show them how to be rich
in the blessings of You
Your merciful grace
forgiveness
and never ending love

show to them Lord
the peace
that is You

<u>Your Most Precious and Holy Word</u>

Help me Lord
find the blessings in Your Word
the gifts and knowledge waiting there
written yes, so long ago
but so very relevant today
Your message of love and truth
not hidden, not lost
but waiting for me to pick up and read
to spend time with You
walking beside You here
listening to You speak to me
knowing that it is the same for all
who will take the time
to sit with You, walk here with You
through Your Holy and precious Word
being gifted with a special understanding
hearing what You would have us each to know
finding Your message, finding Your love

Blessed

over and over again
directed, Lord, to all of Your children
spreading over me Lord
spreading over each and all, Your love
wrapping us in Your peace
blessing me
blessing all
who come to You here Lord
with Your merciful grace and forgiveness
blessing me
blessing all
who come to You Lord
to spend time with You
in Your most precious and holy Word.
Your Word, Your truth, never ending

~~~~~~~~~~~~~~~~~~~~~~~~~~~~

Shine In Me

Shine in me Lord
in everything I do
let Your light glow brightly
allow me to be
a reflection of You

Shine in me Lord
in all that I say
let Your words come forth
in each conversation
every day

Shine in me Lord
through a gentle hand

Rebecca Stepp Revels

give me strength and compassion
so that in every action
all see You, in where I stand

Shine in me Lord
every where that I go
let my all to You be true
so when others look at me
it is You, that they will know

Shine in me Lord
let my all to You be true
so when others look a me
they see You

~~~~~~~~~~~~~~~~~~~~~~~~~~~

<u>Now and Always</u>

Lord,
I am here thinking,
of the multitudes that flocked to You
walking beside You, with You, as You traveled
listening to Your voice as You spoke about Your Father's kingdom.
watching as with a simple word or touch, You healed many
and forgave more
How so many struggled to be close to You
wishing to hear every word
How so many wished just to touch the hem of Your cloak
as You passed them on Your way
they gathered in the homes were You rested
along the roadways, just to see You pass
on the mountainside, and on the banks of the sea
watching for You, wishing to hear You speak to them
I think Lord, of that time, of those multitudes so long ago
longing to have been a part of that

Blessed

knowing though, that my time is now, my place is here
while I could not walk those roads, then, in Your presence Lord
when You lived as man, walking the roads in Your earthly presence
seeing You, being able to reach out and physically touch You
hearing Your voice speaking out, teaching, preaching, forgiving
I do walk with You in faith Lord
I feel You with me, walking beside me, guiding me in my path
Your Spirit dwells with in me and my heart laughs with that joy
I hear You speak to me, in my heart
and I am, a part of the multitude,
that flocks to You, wishing to be close to You
now
and always.

Even in the Moments

How can I describe the joy
that comes even with the tears?
as they course down my face
tracking cheeks yet again
there is a cleansing
there is a peace that comes
from knowing in all things
You are near,
nothing happens that You are unaware
my pain and suffering is not ignored
as You stand at the ready for my call
You wait, for me to come to You
and come to You I will
I know, in all that I am
You are Who I need, only You, can ease my pain
comfort me in all times of suffering
leading me to a place of rest

Rebecca Stepp Revels

giving me chance to regain my strength
to go out and try again
to go out and live again
in a way that will honor You
share You with those that do not know You
trying to put voice, to the things I know
the things that rest safely in my heart
treasured knowledge that brings great joy
even, in the moments of suffering.

Where Fear Meets Faith

I will go out on this day Lord
even in my worries
as the fear attempts to wrap around me
trying to strangle me
knowing what I face
today, steps will be set into motion
soon, I will know
so I go, walking into this
yet I know I am not alone
You will go with me
You will stand beside me
giving me strength to stand
in the face of my fear
I will go, knowing
that where fear meets faith
You are there.

Blessed

I heard Your voice
Your promise given
sealed in a trusting
believing heart.
Today, I go
where fear, meets faith.
Handing the fear
to You
handing the worries
to You
Knowing that no matter what comes
I am not alone
You are with me
always
even in the places
where fear, meets faith.

Always With Me

I speak to You Lord
where ever I may be
for I know in my heart
You are always with me

I whisper Your name
and I tell You my woe
it doesn't matter the place
for You are, where ever I go

I cry in my anguish
of my suffering and plight
knowing that You're close
with Your comforting Light

I yell in my anger
not knowing what else to do
but knowing You hear

Rebecca Stepp Revels

when I yell out, to You

I speak to You Lord
where ever I may be
for I know in my heart
You are always, with me.

~~~~~~~~~~~~~~~~~

<u>Joy In You</u>

When the pain grows
threatening to overtake my strength
when the tears flow
and I fear that in them I will drown
I turn to You Lord
for You know my pain
I cry out to You in my suffering
You reach out to me with a comforting peace
wrapping me in Your calming presence
covering me, in Your love
I feel You Lord
as You take the burden from me
lifting the weight of the pain from my heart
making my way easier
I walk in the warmth of Your light Lord
guided by You, as You make my way easier
as I look to You, trust in You
to be here always, waiting for me to come to You
whether it be in the times of storms and pain
or when I am realizing,
the wondrous things You have done for me
and I just wish with all of my self
to say thank You Lord
When my pain grows Lord
I will turn, and find joy in You

Blessed

<u>In An Understanding of You</u>

Allow the words Lord, that I speak
be words of You
that tell of Your mercy
of how You found me, lost and alone
speaking to my heart
bringing me, into a relationship with You
help me to tell, in a way understood
just how it is that You are my Lord, You are my Savior
as I come to You Lord, in humble gratitude
for every gift and every blessing that You have given
I come to You, with a humble plea
help me Lord, to know what to say
give to me the words that You would have spoken
at any given time, in any given place
remind me Lord, that no matter where I find myself
there You are also, I am never lost from You
You will never abandon me
no matter the storm, no matter the hardships that come
You will never abandon me
no matter the road I take
I know, that you will find me, and lead me back to You
help me Lord, to share that knowledge
so that those who hear, understand
so that those that hear, take the words to their heart
allowing them to grow in understanding
of Your never ending mercy, never ending grace
unfailing love
Allow the words that I speak Lord,
be the words You would have spoken
in an understanding of You

Rebecca Stepp Revels

<u>Rejoice In This Day</u>

Rejoice in this day, celebrate
a very special birth
rejoice in this day, celebrate
this blessing, this peace on earth
rejoice in this day, sing out in praise
for of lowly birth is born a king
rejoice in this day, sing out in praise
a new way He has come to bring
rejoice in this day, shout out in joy
follow the star through the night
rejoice in this day, shout out in joy
find the child asleep, under a heavenly light
rejoice in this day, hallelujah
for unto us a Savior is born
rejoice in this day, hallelujah
born to wear a crown made of thorn
rejoice in this day, celebrate
the Son of God, come to earth as man
rejoice in this day, celebrate
this gift, soon with nail scarred hand
rejoice in this day, sing out
for love has come to every one
rejoice in this day, sing out
for unto us, is born God's Son
rejoice and shout hallelujah
let peace reign across this earth
rejoice and sing hallelujah
for Jesus the Christ, born of lowly birth.

Blessed

Ever Closer Lord

Today, let me walk in Your way
let my footsteps follow Yours
as I walk with You
let me feel You ever closer beside me
guiding me as we walk
show me the gifts
that wait to be seen along the way
slow me down enough to see
allow me to hear the music of the moment
laughter of a child, song of a bird
whisper of I love you, from someone dear
today Lord, let me walk in Your way
feeling You ever closer to me
guiding me, through the trials of this life
to an eternity of peace with You.

~~~~~~~~~~~~~~~~~~~~~~~~~~~~~~

Comfort In You

In the midst of the storm
when the harsh winds blow cold
rain lashes down, pounding all it falls upon
like a thousand needles, stinging and sharp
when the clouds gather thick, covering the sun
blanketing my world in an eerie darkness
sending fear to my heart
thunder rumbles loud and ominous
the tremble it brings I feel to my very core
In the midst of all this
I hear Your voice, softly calling

Rebecca Stepp Revels

like a lost lamb found, I rush to You
finding comfort in the presence of You
knowing that with You, all is well
You quite the tempest of my storms
the very waves hear Your command and obey
the winds still and the stinging rain, a gentle mist
a rinsing away of the fear and pain
I hear You, calling to me
following You, I am lead to a place of rest
the comfort of Your peace wraps around me, soothing me
no worries can get to this place
no fears, no storms can reach it
for it is a place of Your making
here I am safe
wrapped securely
in Your mercy, grace and love
immeasurable and never ending.

My Heart Sings

I feel the song in my heart Lord
a giddy feeling of nothing short of joy
singing for You
for even when my body grows weary
from the trials of this life,
when strength fades for need of rest
my heart sings, with a joy like none other
for it sings, to You Lord
praises for You,
a thanksgiving for the blessings that You give
the gifts of this life, the moments that it is obvious

that You are here, so very close

Blessed

my heart sings, the words written in Your spirit of love
the words a testimony of Your grace
I feel my heart sing and with each note

Your Spirit in me, dances in joyous abandon
for Your love covers all
Your peace gives rest to a weary spirit
Your love, writes the words
that my heart sings
thank you dear sweet Lord
for the songs..

~~~~~~~~~~~~~~~~~~~~~~~~

Into Your Perfect Plan

When I fear Lord, I turn to You
for You did not create in us, this feeling
the one that threatens to overwhelm
the feeling that tries to destroy all hope
but You dear Lord, are my hope
You are my strength and my rock
in You all things are possible
in You all things shall be done as You have planned
When worries Lord, threaten my spirit
I turn to You
my burdens and my cares are lifted by Your hand
as You lead me through the storm
into Your perfect plan

Rebecca Stepp Revels

I will have no fear, as You Lord
are my rock, my salvation, my strength
the light through the darkness
with You, no harm shall come to pass
I place my trust and hope
in You Lord
walking with You, holding tightly to You Lord
as the winds of tribulation blow
as the evils of the day attack
You are my shelter through it all
I trust, in Your perfect plan
When this world threatens,
and it seems too much to bear
I turn to You, my shield and my strength
My Lord.

~~~~~~~~~~~~~~~~~~~~~~~~~~~~~~~

By The Beauty of Your Love

How beautiful is Your love Lord
shining down on me
Your blessings falling freely
through out each and every day
how beautiful is Your love Lord
bringing peace to a worried heart
gracing me with a comforting mercy
no matter the storms that blow
how beautiful is Your love Lord
in the comfort of Your presence
granting me strength
blessing me with peace
guiding me always
by the beauty, of Your love

~~~~~~~~~~~~~~~~~~~~~~~~~~~~~~~

Blessed

<u>Only You Lord</u>

Voices raised to You Lord
prayers for many in need
voices filled with tears
fears of what may come
as they tremble in concern
weighted down, by the worries
falling Lord, to their knees before You
raising hands in supplication
raising voices in prayer
asking for Your presence
asking Lord, for Your comfort
peace Lord, that can only come from You
in times like this
as each cross seems too heavy to bear
dragging in the dust of despair
each soul growing weary in the battle
each step a struggle to take
voices are raised to You Lord
filled with the sound of falling tears
seeking Your provisions
seeking only what You can give
a peaceful comforting love
rest for the weary at heart
voices raised to You Lord
for only You
only You
Yes You Lord
are still in control.

~~~~~~

Rebecca Stepp Revels

<u>I am Blessed</u>

I feel You with me
as the dawning sun rises
greeting a new morn
Your presence, a comfort
a reminder
I am not alone
as I walk this journey called life
I am not alone
as I stand in the winds of the storm
I am not alone
as the seasons change around me
moving on
I am not alone
as I see new life born
and elders, pass on to eternity
I am not alone
as I weep for the injustices
or sing out for the joys
I am comforted
in You sweet Lord
in all things
in all ways
I feel Your presence
when I come to You in need
I feel You close
as You answer my pleas
I am comforted Lord
knowing You
knowing the blessings
of Your grace
feeling the gift of Your mercy
free in the fact
of Your absolute forgiveness

Blessed

as morning dawns anew
a new day
a new chance
to walk with You
I am blessed

<u>I Shout Lord</u>

I shout Lord of Your blessings
that You so graciously provide
covering us in Your blessings
within Your love, I abide
I sing Lord of Your mercy
that You grant Lord, in Your holy way
forgiving us without reservation
of the transgressions we commit each day
I shout Lord of Your presence
and how You are always there
we do not go without You Lord
that knowledge I happily share
I dance Lord with joyous abandon
at the blessings you have given me
and knowing Lord the time will come
I'll be forever with You, in eternity

Rebecca Stepp Revels

I Know You Lord

I hear Your voice Lord
and I will not be afraid
as You speak to me
calling to me
reminding me, that You are here
whether I stand on the hillside
watching
and Your voice calls to me
or if I walk through the valleys and storms
I know
You are with me,
You will guide me always
through the darkness
You will laugh with me in the sunlight
and dance with me in the rain
splashing in the puddles of Your creation
I fear You not Lord
even when I am reminded of my errors
even when Your Spirit lets me know
when I have erred in my actions
it is with Your loving hand that I am corrected
guided back to where I need be
I know You Lord
and I fear You not
for I feel Your presence
I feel Your great love
in every moment of my life
I feel You
walking with me every step of this journey
I know You Lord
and You know me
better than I know myself
forgiving me
guiding me

Blessed

loving me
I am thankful always
that I know You Lord.

Christ Is Born

Do you hear
the songs of the angels
as they sing, hallelujah?

Christ is born

Do you see
the shepherds as they search
for this new born King

Christ is born

Do you see
as the shepherds bow in reverence
then run to tell

Christ is born

Do you hear
the joyous shouting
of those that understand

Christ is born

Do you know
that it is prophecy fulfilled
on this day that

Christ is born.

Rebecca Stepp Revels

Hallelujah

As the bells ring out
we shout hallelujah   Hosanna
for on this day of great joy
comes to us a gift
in the form of a baby boy
blessed Hosanna
sing praise to the King
a promise fulfilled
as the angels sing
come to us, to show the way
born to us of lowly birth
this heavenly King of Kings you see
residing now on earth
bells ring out
and the angles sing
hallelujah hallelujah
tonight is born the King

Blessed

<u>In You Lord</u>

I trust You Lord, in all things
You are the Light, that guides me
through the darkest of times
though the storm clouds gather
I fear not, for I trust in You
You are my shield and my protector
In You, I am safe
though the winds and rains batter me
causing me to stumble and fall
the cold of the night, causing me to tremble
I worry not,
for You are here Lord, You are my comfort
You are my shelter
in You, I am safe
When my soul feels empty
I hunger for knowledge of You
to know you better
as Lord, and as friend
Your Word feeds my hunger
Your Word quenches my thirst
for You are the Bread of Life
You are the Living Water
in You, I am filled
In those moments Lord
when I feel alone
Your comfort comes
Your peace wrapping around me
Your love blankets me
calming my spirit, healing my pains
With You, in You, I find rest from my storms
I find Your spirit that fills my emptiness
I find Your merciful grace
in the forgiveness You give so freely
in You Lord, I am loved

Rebecca Stepp Revels

<u>My Sweet Lord</u>

Sweet Lord
how I praise Your name
for the blessings
You have given me
Sweet Lord
how I love You
for You walk with me
as a friend
Sweet Sweet Lord
how I thank You
for all things that I know
come directly from You
You bless me
with Your presence
Your comfort
and the all encompassing peace
that blankets my life
Sweet Lord
I thank you
Blessed Lord
I thank You
for You have given me much
asking only that I believe
asking, that I trust fully
in a walk with You
and I do Lord
for Your love is all I need
Your love is all I want
Sweet Lord, I thank You
for Your grace and merciful forgiveness
gives to me a peace
that can only come from You
My sweet Lord.

Blessed

<u>Your Peace Unfolding</u>

With a year that began, in a way unexpected
fears unfolding like new blanket
covering the bed of this moment
with feelings unknown before
I stood in the dawn of greater belief
growing brighter, as faith rises like the sun
its intensity stronger, better
with each moment of trial
Nights of fear, evaporated in the moonlight of Your love
showing them to be nothing of concern
giving me more cause to believe and to trust
moments of exhaustion, leaving me weak
fragile in person, You come to me
giving to me a rest for the soul
gifting me with moments of peace
that bring with them, strength needed to continue
in all things, You have been with me
during all things, I trusted in You
waited on Your time
now, Your time has been met
and in the evening of the year
as the sun begins its slow climb from the sky
I know, the faith I have held tightly
gives to me blessings from You
and You have taken that blanket of fear and concern
away from the bed of this time
replacing it with a comforter
of Your healing peace and love.

Rebecca Stepp Revels

Greatest of All Things

I come to You
on bended knee
wishing to offer up a humble prayer
thank you dear Lord
for Your blessings
You provide for us in all ways
gifting us, in ways undeserved
we need not,
for we have You
we want not
for You so freely give
I fear not
for Your promise never ends
I come to You Lord
in humble thanks
knowing
as You take care of the sparrow
as You clothe the lily of the field
You take care of us
and the greatest of all things given
is Your love.

Blessed

<u>Your Love Conquers All</u>

Through the darkest of the storms
You guide us
when we stand on the brink of disaster
famine strikes our land and our heart
when we seek but know not what
questions without answers
problems without resolutions
as fears take hold of our heart
and we hide, trembling in the dark
when we fight alone against the worries of the day
leaving us weak and weary
hungry for physical needs
hungry, unknowingly, for spiritual needs
You are our answer
yet we try, to go alone
fighting to prove we are our own strength
when in truth, we are our greatest weakness
fears over come us
unable to win, we attempt to run
finding no comfort in the darkness
our tears flow in our desperation
as finally, finally on bended knee
we seek You
the One who was there, all along
waiting
reaching out your hand of grace
You guide us to a place of rest
blanketing us in a comforting peace
feeding our soul with Your Spirit
You secure us in Your mercy and love
in You, there is no fear
for Your love, conquers all.

Rebecca Stepp Revels

<u>You</u>

How do I explain
what words do I use
that will adequately describe
You?
Some believe, they understand
the words they've heard
all along
Others scoff and laugh
arguing, denying
You
What words, do I use
to all in which I converse
that will show
You
the One that I know
have in my life
granting me, gifting me
with a pure peace
Your love flowing down
onto me
how do I explain
how do I show
just how close You are
I ask You Lord
when the words do not come
when I try to speak
when I can not accurately convey
You
allow the actions
of You, shining through
do it for me
bringing glory Lord only
to You

Blessed

<u>I Hear Your Voice</u>

I heard Your voice, calling me
a heart cold and hard, callous from life
I heard Your voice and I tried to ignore the sound
as I struggled in the dark, fighting enemies seen and unseen
fighting myself most of all
as I battled desires of earthly origin

Slugging through a path of mud
sinking into muck of misery
weary of the journey I chose
yet not knowing the way out of the dark

shrieks and cries of pure evil sounded around me
claws of creatures lurking in the night reach out to me
my soul crying out in deep despair
feeling so very lost in the depths of misery
falling, crumbling to the ground beneath my feet
hearing the wail that escapes from my lips
as the suffering of my stubbornness becomes too much

I hear Your voice
calling to me, speaking to my wounded heart
offering a light out of the darkness
offering hope in the place of my despair
offering healing, in the stead of my pain
offering so much, if I but hear and answer

Hanging my head in shame I hear another voice
whispering angrily, in a manner vile and ugly
reminding me, of the things I have done
the ways I have acted, words I have said
In my shame, I threatened to turn away

Rebecca Stepp Revels

unworthy, the voice hissed, you are unworthy

but Your voice, spoke to me once more
a voice of nothing but love
reaching out to me
offering me a gift like none other
a gift that no one else, could give
in the act of greatest mercy
a gift of grace

I hear Your voice, and I turn to You
I see Your light shining through the darkness
and I follow
finding the most blessed gift of all
given in Your love
the simple gift,
of forgiveness.

~~~~~~~~~~~~~~~~~~~~~~~~~~~~~~~~

I Feel You

I feel You
walking with me
sharing with me all moments
of this journey
You know all of my needs
as we travel
I feel You
holding me when I cry
comforting me
when fears grow
sheltering me
when the storms rage
I feel You
walking with me
sharing with me, all moments
and I am glad.

Blessed

<u>How I Love You Lord</u>

How I love You Lord
excited, overjoyed in Knowing You
for You are my joy
comforting me in my worst times
when the fears
and the tears threaten to overwhelm
sheltering me
when the storms reach their peak
and the waves are rising
swamping this boat of life
calming them with Your presence
and a word
How Lord, that I love You
when You remind me often
patiently, how You are near
always near
showing me the beauty
pointing out the gifts of Your love
I feel Your presence
beside me guiding
in my heart residing
in my soul abiding
and the storms have no chance
the fears, the tears no sustenance
as Your love wraps around me
blessing me
with a peace and a love
immeasurable.
How I do love You Lord

Rebecca Stepp Revels

<u>I Will Trust</u>

I know Lord
that even though You walk with me
this road is not easy
it is not meant to be
each storm, each trial
a lesson in strength, patience
a way, for me to move closer to You
finding and learning the truth
that there are times
the bad things that happen
do so to bring us to our greatest moments
so that we see Your hand in all things
and in them, give to You the glory
I know, that this journey
will have moments that I do not understand
but I will trust in You Lord
to give to me all that I will need
to walk with me at all times
as I make my way
to eternity with You.

Blessed

<u>The Music of Your Love</u>

Smiling I raise my arms to You Lord
dancing in the music of Your love
twirling and spinning childlike
to the song of Your peace
Your love flows through me
wrapping around me
as a song oft sung
as a blanket of warmth
on a cool day, I feel You here
as a cool mountain spring
on a hot summer morn, I feel You
close to me
laughing with me
as I dance to the music of Your love
fears have no chance
worries no hold
as You lead me by the hand
to a shelter, built by You, waiting for me
a place of rest, of rejuvenation
a place, where I can dance
to the music of Your love
for this time, there is no cross to bear
for this time, burdens are set aside
my soul is replenished in Your word
my song of praise for You rings loud
for I know in You
with You here by my side
I can dance happily, I can dance freely
without fear
to the music of Your love

Rebecca Stepp Revels

For The Lost

Under the bridges they reside
in the woods, in the back alleys they hide
sleeping in a box or out in the street
never making eye contact, with those they meet
lost
with no home to call their own
struggling, stumbling through this life they roam
hungry of soul, hungry at heart
needing something, not sure where to start
lost
suffering, not knowing how much more they can bear
wondering does anyone know they are there
as they sit on a curb, hunger an enemy, never a friend
as they despair of ways, to make it end
lost
running from some one, or some terrible thing
not sure of what, tomorrow may bring
thinking it has to be better, than what they left behind
cold, hunger and loneliness, what they find
lost
many, so many walk the street
not looking in the eyes, of those they meet
empty of soul, empty of heart
wishing to live, don't know where to start
lost
hold out a hand of compassion and love
act as the Savior, looks down from above
reach out in caring, shown the love that you can
be like the One, with the nail scarred hand
for the lost.
remember that once, You were there too

Blessed

remember just what, He did for you
taking some things, yet giving you much more
when you answered His knock, as He stood at the door
lost
we were lost, each in our own way
until we heard, the Savior on that day
when He called to each of us by name
nothing, no nothing, is ever the same
saved.
loved
forgiven

Rain of His Love

Standing in the rain, feeling it falling down upon me
gently rolling off my cheeks
washing away feelings of the day
I stand with face upraised
smiling into the falling rain, tasting the drops on my lips
closing my eyes to the moment as I simply feel
the scent of the rain falling around me, fresh and new
cleansing the air, and the land,
rinsing the day's moments from me
on the outside
On the inside my heart is rinsed in the saving grace
my soul in the mercies of the Lord
on the inside, I stand with face upraised
looking toward the source of love
feeling the dark of my life washed away
by the One true Light
on the inside, my spirit shines, as forgiveness granted
lifts away the weights of my transgressions
I am a new person, I am changed, redeemed in my Lord
washed in the blood of my Savior
with face and hands upraised, I stand in the falling rain of His love.

Rebecca Stepp Revels

<u>For The Least of These</u>

For those that search
wandering lost and alone
answers so very difficult to find
when they do not understand
what it is they seek.
Questions go through their minds
pain in their heart
as the road is so dark
the way so cold
stumbling along, alone
sounds come from the darkness
temptations call out from all sides
it would be so easy to give in,
some do, some struggle on
illness and loneliness a constant companion
despair burdens the heart
as they seek answers, to questions they do not know
empty eyes look out onto a world
people passing, turning away
will no one reach out a compassionate hand
as the Master would do, would expect one to
for the least, for the lost, for the lonely
who are seeking answers
to the questions they do not know.

Blessed

Your Whisper

I hear Your whisper, speaking to my heart
calming my inner storms
taking me to a place of security
in the arms of Your peace
giving me a place of rest
when around me there is nothing but worries
a struggle to move on
to continue on a journey in a life difficult
I hear You whisper my name
reminding me, You know me
are close to me, through all things
wrapping me in a blanket of Your grace
letting me know, that in Your forgiveness
I have a peace that can come from nowhere else
I have a promise, You will never leave me
That at the end of this journey
I will go home to You
I have the peace of Your love
when I hear Your whisper.

Rebecca Stepp Revels

<u>In Your Time</u>

No matter where You send me Lord
no matter what I face
I know that I will not face it alone
for You are with me
At my side always, giving to me the strength
to continue on the journey
that You have set for me

As I go Lord, lead me, so that my steps are true
that I know which path to take along the way
guide me Lord, through the dark of the storm
to Your safe harbor of rest
Strengthen me Lord I ask, so that I may carry
the cross that is mine to bear

As I go, where You send me
knowing, You have a plan for me
I ask that I hear You, when You speak
understanding, what it is You wish
and that with strength given by You
I will accomplish what You plan
in Your time.

Blessed

<u>Walking a Road</u>

You walked a road knowing
what waited at its end
the pain that would be inflicted
upon Your body in flesh
understanding that it had to be
not Your will, but the Father's
a lamb of sacrifice
to save a fallen world
You walked, explaining the Way
the only way to Heaven's door
to the throne of the Most High
and You were rejected
as You knew would happen
beaten, scourged and crucified
and yet, nailed to the cross
You asked for forgiveness for those
that were responsible for putting You there.
Laid in a tomb, wrapped in burial cloth
those that knew You wept
not understanding, that this had to be
not comprehending, how this would set me free
up from that grave You arose
hallelujah Lord, You arose
and Satan at that moment lost

I walk a road knowing
what lies at the end
a Savior waiting, with arms open wide
welcoming me home
because You knew Lord
what had to be
not Your will
but the Father's
whose grace
mercy and love

Rebecca Stepp Revels

freely
offers forgiveness
redemption
for those that accept.

And More

I am here again Lord
coming to You
down on my knees
weary
tired of fighting
struggling to walk
in a life that can be so hard
I am here again Lord
with down cast eyes
knowing that I have done wrong
weary
of battling on my own
needing You
I am here Lord
with tears flowing freely
fears and worries
overflow my soul
so I bring them to You Lord
lay them at Your feet
knowing that You
will give me strength of heart
peace of soul
to bear this cross
knowing that You
will walk along side
and when the weight gets too much
You will lift me up
carry me in Your arms
as I rest in You

Blessed

I am here Lord
despairing in the ugliness of my wrongs
overcome by the weakness of will
the frailty of this body
knowing there is comforting strength in You
knowing there is forgiveness for all, in You
I come to You Lord
thanking You
for all these things
and more.

Journey To You

Help me dear Lord,
to always look to You
for You are my strength
my shield against this life
as I journey to You
let me not worry nor even see
what snares are planted in my path
to cause me concern
to attempt to bring me down
weaken my testimony to You
be my shield Lord
against the stress that can come
each and every moment of the day here
protect me from the evil one and his efforts
protect me, from my own fears
walk with me I pray Lord
guide me along this path to You
help me to keep my eyes to You
and only You Lord
neither looking right or left
for there is nothing there

Rebecca Stepp Revels

that can do for me as You do Lord
teach me in this walk Your mercy
that I may show it to others as I go
offering a compassionate hand
to those in need
help me Lord
that I do not see, what I do not have
for there are those who have even less
help me that I may offer what I can
open my heart to them
that in the sharing of physical needs
I offer a seed to the spiritual
be with me, walk with me, guide me
on this journey to You
for You are all I need.

~~~~~~~~~~~~~~~~~~~~~~~~~~~~~~~

There Is

There is a point
a place in time
when it all will end
There is a door
waiting
to be opened up
for those who heard the call
to enter in
There is a Savior
calling
speaking to one and all
calling
the falling
There is coming a time
for it all to be done

Blessed

the saints will be called home
to Heaven's shore
There is
a time approaching fast
when this life
will be completed
and we will meet in a place
where there will be pain
no more
There is
I believe in this
I trust in this
I wait, as I travel
for this
There is a time
that will be here soon
when this life on earth is done
I will not miss
there is
coming
a time

I am ready

~~~~~~~~~~~~~~~~

As We Travel

'Tis but a fleeting moment
this life
each day unique
never to be here again
visited only in memory
as we pass along this road
taking this journey
to where ever it will lead us

Rebecca Stepp Revels

it is up to us to decide
the way in which we will travel
will we walk, with our eyes straight ahead
seeing only the path before us
not looking to either side
refusing to see
what may distract us from our goal
will we walk,
with our hands closed tightly
held at our side
not reaching out
for that may slow us
will we walk
with our hearts and our minds
closed?
Refusing to allow them to feel and understand
for that may deter us
from what we have planned.

Or will we walk
in the way of the Savior
treading slowly along the pathway
looking to the sides of the way
for those that are lost
stumbling along the outside
that do not know the way
will we hear their cries
opening our hands reaching out
reaching for them
to bring them closer
lift them up from the trenches
will we see their afflictions
understand their pain

opening our hearts in compassion
as the Savior would
as the Savior does

Blessed

through us
should we allow

as we travel this journey
on our way
to our destination

~~~~~~~~~~~~~~~~~~~~~~~~~~~

<u>You Are My Lord</u>

You are my warmth Lord
when the days are cold

You are my Light
in the darkness

You are my Comforter
when the worries of this life come

You are my Safe Harbor
in the midst of storms

You are my Strength
when I grow weary

You are the Living Water
when I thirst

You are the Bread of Life
Your word, food for my soul

You are my Lord
my Salvation

You are my Lord

Rebecca Stepp Revels

my life

You are my Lord
Your mercy freely given

Your grace offered openly
undeserved, unearned

You are my Lord
You have redeemed me

You have forgiven me
You have given me life anew
in You

You are my Lord.

~~~~~~~~~~~~~~~~~~~~~~~

In You

In You
I need not fear
for Your love
guides me
through all
and I know
that I am safe
in You

~~~~~~~~~~~~~~~~~~~~~~~

Blessed

With You

I stand here Lord
on the threshold of a new day
dawn yet not here
I look before me wondering
what this day will bring
what waits
but I hold no fear
harbor no worries
for I know, with all that I am
You walk with me
You stand by me in all things
any storm that blows
rain that falls
You are my shelter
protecting me along the way
there is no darkness too deep
that You cannot guide me through
so I hold no fear
no enemy can harm me
for even should it be
that they destroy this earthly body
my spirit will soar to You
at Your feet Lord
I will rest
my journey then done
until then, I will stand at the ready
look out upon each new dawn
ready for this walk with You
knowing, You are beside me
showing me all the things
that You have placed along the way
showing me all the things
that I could do, for You
so that the ones along the way
may see You as well.

Rebecca Stepp Revels

I stand here Lord
at the threshold of this new day
and I smile as I wonder
what this new day will bring
with You.

<u>The Peace That is You</u>

How can I explain Lord
the peace that I have
that comes from You?

Simple words are not enough
for words are easily ignored
misunderstood

Elaborate words can confuse
cause listeners to turn away
frustrated

I want to share Lord
the feelings I have
inside my heart

How Lord
show me the way
to show You

in my walk with You
as I talk with You
show me, so that I may share

and so that others may know
in their heart as well
the peace, that is You.

Blessed

Hope

to trust in You Lord
is my hope
my belief that all will be well
storms will come
bringing winds of worry and fear
You are my rock
my strength and my shelter
You are my hope
that tomorrow will be better
You are my guide
leading me to a place of rest
when the journey gets long
when the cross that I bear
grows heavy
and this body grows weary
You take me to a place of peace
giving me a time to understand
that in the storms is growth
growing closer to You
in belief in You
in faith in You
You are my Savior
my Lord and my Rock
in You
there is hope.

Rebecca Stepp Revels

It Is a Joy

It is a joy to serve You Lord
through out my every day
hoping that my actions
are Yours in every way
my words are Yours in compassion
gently may I speak
giving others hope and faith
You're the answer that they seek
keep me strong in Your path
as on this life I journey through
keep me steadfast and strong
on this mission I have to You
It is a joy to serve You Lord
give me the strength I pray
that no matter what may come Lord
I am faithful in every way
seeing the poor around me
be they hungry, sick or cold
give me a way to ease their suffering
that speaks of You clear and bold
give me eyes to see the lost
and a heart wise enough to care
give me the words of direction
and the fire, to stop and share
It is a joy to serve You Lord
use me as You may
allow me to sing Your praises
every moment, of every day.

Blessed

<u>The Gift of Your Morning</u>

In the morning sun, rising
I see Your smile
the gift of a new day
there is a peace here
a contentment of the things that are
an anticipation, of the things that will be
as life wakes and begins again
I hear the wildlife around me as they stir
the colors of the land brighten in the light
it is indeed a gift, this present of the present
as I open the day, I look to the opportunity before me
knowing, my actions are my choice
I choose to act as You would have me to act Lord
I know that You are with me, always beside me
help me that my words all be gentle
flavored with Your kindness and love
help me that my actions be of compassion
a reaching out to those in need of a hand up
help me, that all I do, be of You
practicing Your merciful grace in all things
understanding that even in the glory of a new dawn
there is always chance for the storm
should someone speak less kindly
react less lovingly
help me to understand with compassionate patience
as You would
help me Lord, to allow this storm to pass
all the while handling the breaking waves as You would
in the hopes that those whose days are less bright
will see You
as a light shining through me
so that they too, will find the glory
the peace and redemption
in You Lord

so that they too, will see the beauty
will open their eyes and hands
to the gift of a new day's dawn
and know, it was given in love, by You.

Time Grows Short

I stand at the ready
looking for You Lord
watching for You
knowing, time is short

I look to the morning
watching the sunrise
another day to wait
could You come today?

I go through time seeking You,
while seeking to share You
every day
with those that I meet, along the way

I stand at the ready
looking down this road I travel
watching for those yet lost
reaching out a compassionate hand

offering Your words to all who will hear
hoping that they understand
that time grows short
In my heart I know, Your return is near

I offer to all Your message
of understanding, mercy and love

Blessed

I seek to share Your gift
of forgiveness for the things we are guilty of

I will travel on this journey
through a life that is growing short
acting in this life as You would have me
so that it is not me, but You they see

for I look at the morning sun
at a day beginning anew
understanding that times grows short
and soon, we will be with You.

~~~~~~~~~~~~~~~~~~~~~~~~~~~~~~

In These Things

In the kiss and caress of a gentle breeze
the soft blanket of the morning sun
the touch of a loved ones hand
I feel You
In the laughter of the river, splashing happily on its way
the song of nature in it's many tenors
in the coo of a contended child
I hear You
in the brilliant pallet of the setting sun
the rainbow of colors in a field of flowers
in mountains majestic, and seas vast and wild
I see You
in the whisper in my heart reminding me
the touch to my soul assuring me
the feeling of Your presence beside me
I know You
and in all things
I thank You my Lord

Rebecca Stepp Revels

<u>I Will Hold No Fear</u>

The storm clouds are slowly building
gathering once again
yet I will not fear their coming
for You are here
walking beside me
here to guide me
through the roughest of the winds
sheltering me always
from the most fierce of the rains
walking beside me, whispering to my heart
singing comforting songs to my soul
giving me strength when my cross grows heavy
giving me rest, when this body grows weary
so I fear not
what things may come
I will allow them to worry me not
for You are with me
walking beside me
bringing me comfort in the storms
reassurance in Your love
hope arisen in Your merciful grace
unearned
I will hold no fear
of the storm clouds that gather
of the winds that begin to blow
for I know that You are with me
that's all I need to know.

Blessed

<u>A Little Closer Lord</u>

Just a little closer Lord
let me walk with You
just a little closer
in every thing I do
allow me to feel Your presence
brushing against my hand
just a little closer
as I cross a barren land
Just a little closer Lord
walk closer Lord with me
so when dark storm clouds come
Your Light is all I see
Just a little closer Lord
be settled in my heart
so that in every emotion
You have a part
Just a little closer
walk with You every day
being a little closer
as I walk Your holy way
Just a little closer Lord
I want to be to You
feeling Your loving presence
in everything I do
Just Lord, Just a little closer
walk this journey with me
take this life and make it Yours
so that You, is what others see
walking a little closer Lord
closer Lord, to me.

Rebecca Stepp Revels

<u>Let My Understanding Grow</u>

Let my understanding Lord
of You grow
spreading in my heart
showing in my life
grant me wisdom of You
so that I can share
plant a seed of understanding
in the hearts of those I meet
plant a seed of longing
in those without You
Share with me Lord
so that I may in turn share
the love that is You

Let my understanding grow Lord
of Your holy and awesome ways

Let my understanding grow
of Your mercy, love and grace

Let my understanding grow Lord
in all things that are You
so that it is You I glorify
in all the things I do

Let my understanding grow Lord
as I walk with You
allow me to share Your glory
let it be You that is shining through

Blessed

Let my understanding grow Lord
while in the storms that I pass through
You will guide my life
if I but give it all to You

Let my understanding grow Lord
is my daily prayer
grant me understanding
so I can tell others, how You care

Let my understanding grow Lord
is my daily prayer
grant me the words I need
to tell others, You are there

Let my understanding grow
in everything I do
of Your awesomeness and wonder
in everything that's You

Wrapped In Your Love

Wrapped in Your love Lord
held in Your arms
safe from all worries
safe from all harm
wrapped in Your love
knowing peace full and true
rest for the weary
given by You
wrapped in Your forgiveness
held tightly and strong
reassured of that promise
when I slip and do wrong
wrapped in Your peace
comforted by Your mercy
knowing in my heart
You're always there for me
wrapped in Your presence
held tight by Your grace
assured You are with me
while I travel this place
wrapped in You Lord
I seek always to be
until the time comes
when Your face I see.

Blessed

<u>Let it Show</u>

Let it show in me
Your love
how You walk with me
in this world
as I travel Lord
to You
Let it show in me
Your peace
living in me
as I give to You
every storm
that comes
Let it show in me
Your compassion
and let me
as I walk
show the same
to others
Let it show in me Lord
Your forgiveness
of the mistakes that I make
so that I can share
Your merciful grace
with others
Let it show Lord in me
Your enduring peace
merciful grace
forgiving redemption
all encompassing love
show
So that others
will see that You are real
You are here
always
with open arms

Rebecca Stepp Revels

> welcoming
> Your children
> home.

~~~~~~~~~~~~~~~~~~~~~~~~~~~~~~~~~~~~

<u>I Know that I Know</u>

I know
that I know
that I know dear Lord
You are in my life

I know
that I know
that I know
You are my Lord
My Savior
In You I am complete

I know
that I know
that I know
You have rescued me
brought me out of a darkness

forgiven me, redeemed me from my sins
set me free

I know
that I know
that I know, Sweet Lord
Your comforting rest, when I am weary
Your sheltering arms in the storm
I am safe...in You

Blessed

I know
that I know
that I know Your presence
I hear Your voice speaking to me
I feel You move in my heart
and I know
that I know
that I know
You.

~~~~~~~~~~~~~

<u>I Hear You Lord</u>

I hear You Lord,
speaking to me
Your voice
a gentle song in my heart
encouraging me
inviting me
to walk ever closer
to You Lord.
I hear Your voice
speaking to me
reminding me
how near to me
You are.
Your voice Lord
the most beautiful of music
a song of the greatest love
immeasurable
unending
I hear You Lord
and my soul
trembles with joy
at the sound

Rebecca Stepp Revels

<u>I Hear You</u>

You spoke to the disciples so long ago
instructing them, to go and tell
share Your word among the world
tell them of You, how You are the Way
You said to go, and be a Light
to You, to Heaven's door
for You Lord, are that door
In my heart I see You
speaking to Peter, asking
"Do You love me? then feed my sheep."
but it was not just Peter You instructed
it is all who believe and trust
who are instructed, to go and tell
in Your loving and gentle way
explain, share, be a light
to a dark world
I hear Your voice Lord, speaking
pleading for Your children
to be the Light, that You wish us to be
using gentle word, compassionate hand
to break bread with those who are lost
to share Your Living Water.
I feel You Lord, in Your joy
when one of Your children, find their way
to You, and everlasting life
through Your redemption, Your loving mercy
I hear You speak Lord
and my heart weeps with joy, in knowing You
which is why Lord, I seek to follow Your will
and go and tell.

Blessed

<u>You Speak</u>

You speak
and the seas obey
winds calm

You speak
and the lame are healed
the blind see

You speak
my heart trembles
my soul sings

You speak
and it is good
thank You Lord.

Rebecca Stepp Revels

You Pick Me Up

When my heart cries out
and I fall to my knees
raising my hands to You
reaching out Lord, to You
I have reached the bottom Lord
there is no further to fall
I reach out, crying to You
my strength, gone
When You know, it is fully up to You
all glory goes to You
then You reach out to me
and make me strong
when I have run out of things
that I can do
all my attempts have failed
I turn to You
You hear my cries
see my fears
You pick me up
and dry my tears
When my heart cries out
to my knees I fall
You see my misery
hear my call
and You lift me up
make me strong
here in Your Light
where I belong.

Blessed

<u>You Called My Name</u>

You give to me Lord, all I need
for You are that all
You reached out to me
called my name
brought me close to You
safe in You
I do not walk alone now
for You are ever at my side, ever with me
Your peace comforts me
Your presence guides me
in my words and actions
You show me Lord the wonders
that You have created
the gifts of Your majesty
from the smallest
to that of the largest size
You created all
You are an awesome God
You are Love
in Your great merciful grace,
offering forgiveness
if we but reach out and accept
in turn all You ask
is to go and tell
share, You
share Your love
share, Your peace
You called my name Lord
You called my name
in humility, and in joy
I answered

Rebecca Stepp Revels

<u>Blessed</u>

You have blessed me Lord
as undeserving as I am
many things I have
that are a gift from You
for it is only through You
that all things come.
You have blessed me Lord
in the peace of the early morning light
pushing away the night
bringing a new day, another chance
to be a light for You
You have blessed me Lord
in the many things placed in my responsibility
given the opportunity, to show You
as I go about this day
to show You, in how I act, what I say
to share Your word and Your way
You have blessed me Lord
by calling me to You
offering to me Your blessed forgiveness
undeserved mercy and love
given freely, to me, to all
given, offered, waiting
for us to reach out and receive
so that all
will be blessed
You have blessed me Lord
in ways too numerous to count
I see them Lord, always
and I know, some times, I forget
some times, I take for granted
but I see Lord
and in my heart, I say
thank you

Blessed

<u>As You Move</u>

Tears flow freely
joy so very real
a heart that jumps
as You move
in my life
and the lives of others
With each day
when one comes to You
joy is real
as lives are changed
my soul sings joyously
gloriously to You
as You move
When Your Light shines
on those that are lost
showing them the way, Your Way
from the darkness
out of the sadness and misery
of not knowing
brightening their way
as You move
When Your love
reaches out
blankets all of those that know
warms the hearts
comforts the lives
of Your children
giving them peace
granting them rest
blessing them to share
as You move.

Rebecca Stepp Revels

<u>Grace, Mercy, Forgiveness, Love</u>

Your words touch my heart
leading me
instructing me
to walk this path I take
on this journey to You
acting as You would
my spirit filled with Yours
sings with joy at Your presence
I feel You, filling me
with the love that is You
I hear You in my heart
Your voice of love, tender and gentle
reminding me, to care for the least
to seek the lost, for they are in need
to seek the poor, for they are without
You lead me, showing me, Your children
asking me, instructing me
act as You, be as You
in caring for them
for the least of these are Yours, are You
as I in this place, show Your light and Your love
I feel Your presence in my life
the joy I feel, I wish to share
the peace I have, I offer
for it is not mine to keep
but to offer as a gift, one that grows
spreading as the morning light,
bringing a new day
a new way
I hear Your words
instructing me, teaching me

Blessed

reminding me, to seek those without
to share with those that do not know
have not the understanding
offer to them, what has been so freely given to me
Your unending, immeasurable, all encompassing
grace
mercy
forgiveness
love

<u>I Will Wait Lord</u>

I will wait Lord
on You, on Your time
for what is to come
for from You, blessings flow
from You, peace grows

I will wait Lord
knowing, above all
You are in control of all
the storms that darken the night
attempting to hide Your Light

I will wait Lord
on You, for in Your wisdom
You know, the plan You have
for the one and the all
that answer Your call

I will wait Lord
I will wait, with understanding
that while all things I do not know
I know Your love, mercy and grace
that I hold, while I walk this place

Rebecca Stepp Revels

I will wait Lord
with a patience from You
for the time to come
when I will leave this land of the living
and go home to You, one of the forgiven

~~~~~~~~~~~~~~~~~

I Hear Your Voice

In the silence of the day
I heard Your voice
speaking to me,
calling me to come see
what it was that You have given
the blanket of white covered all
the silence overwhelming
covering all, but the sound of You
listening, I stand in awe
smiling, at the evidence of Your glory
comforted, in the evidence
of Your presence.
as in the silence of the day
I hear Your voice.

Blessed

<u>Seeking You</u>

How soon Lord, how soon
will it be that You return?
I look to the sky Lord
seeking You
anticipating, Your return
how soon?
How much longer Lord, must we wait
for Your return
appearing in the sky, calling our names
seeking us, that are seeking You
How long Lord, how long?
before You return for Your children
as we look to the sky
seeking You
How long Lord, will it be
until You return for Your church
while we wait Lord
give us strength to do Your work
spreading Your word
showing Your way
being a light for You
a light ever seeking You
showing Your glory
as we wonder how long
we do not grow faint in the journey
we do not grow weary in the walk
we toil tirelessly for You Lord
walking without fear into the darkest of places
knowing You are with us
as we reach for those
that do not know You
as we seek You
seeking to do, as You asked
while we wait
wondering, how long Lord, how long?

Rebecca Stepp Revels

You Have Seen

when I am at my worst Lord
You see me
know my struggles
understand my pains
hear the sobs of my heart
see me, fall to my knees
pleading, praying
You see me
You hear my cries
understanding the loneliness I feel
the darkness of the storms
in Your love
You reach out, wrapping me safely
in the security of Your peace
wrapping me, in Your compassionate mercy
in Your redeeming grace
that gives me rest
Your Light, shines out, and the darkness flees
and my tears, cease to be
as again, prayers are answered
and Your love, abounds
for You have seen me at my worst
and in Your love,
brought out, my best.

Blessed

<u>When</u>

When the rains come, and the storm winds blow
I will not fear
for You are my shelter, You are the rock of my life
In You Lord, I am safe
When the heart and soul hungers
I turn to You
and I am fed on Your word
You love fills me and I want no more
When I cry, You comfort me
giving me peace
forgiving me of failings
trespasses against others
redeeming me, making me new
When
I feel alone
You let me know, You are here
always with me
granting me all things
and I am at peace.

Rebecca Stepp Revels

<u>Always</u>

When I listen

when I take the time
make the time

to simply stop
spending quiet time Lord
with You

I hear You

When I walk

with You in this place
You have given me

taking time to listen
I hear You speak
and I see the beauty

You are showing me

When I open my heart

I feel You
living there
healing me

redeeming me from what I was
to be what You need
forgiving me, all things

always

Blessed

<u>Busy</u>

am I busy for You Lord
or just busy
do I fill my days
with thoughts of You
prayers to You
of what You would have me do?
do I see the things
I need to
or merely want to?
Do I see Your children in pain
having needs, that in some way
I can help
do I see them Lord
or am I too busy
am I walking to You Lord
keeping my path straight
my feet my way true
to You
or am I simply walking
no knowing or caring
where this path may take me
am I making the journey
that You would have me make
doing, what You ask of me
or am I too busy
being busy?

Rebecca Stepp Revels

<u>Along This Path</u>

We do not know, how long we have
how long this journey will be
that You Lord, have sent us on
as we make our way to You
the roads that are waiting
which turn to take
will we understand,
to look for what lies around the bend
watching, for the opportunities
You provide
will we see, with our eyes and our heart
what is before us
will we, then act, as You would Lord
help me Lord, along this path
that my eyes are open to see
my ears hear, not only Your instructions
not only Your words
but the cries of those in need
the cries of the lonely, the lost
the cries of Your children, that You have placed in my path
giving me the blessed opportunity
to serve You, by serving them
help me Lord, bless me, give to me
a heart filled with Your compassion
a heart that over flows with Your love
As I continue Lord, along this path set before me
give to me the strength of faith
that others can see
that others who see, will understand
that it comes from You
and the mountains of cold hearts
will be moved.

Blessed

<u>Because of Your Love</u>

They go Lord, out into Your fields
seeking the lost, seeking those that have not heard
They go into the places that are dangerous to be
go into places, so that others may see
the love that is You
They share to the ones they find
Your words, Your way
the blessings that come from knowing You
as well as the warnings, that knowing You
being Your child, is not easy
persecution comes, to one who believes
and dares to live it
They go Lord, because they heard Your voice
speaking to them, calling them, asking them, to go
for You have children that do not know Your voice
You have need of us Lord, to go, to share
for it is not just in far away places
lands of wars and famines that have not heard
there are those just outside our door
who seek something they know not what, or who
they hear You calling, but know not who You are
There are those Lord, that hear You, that know
and who turn away, because they do not understand
or Lord, they are misinformed, or worse
caused to turn away, by those professing to be Yours, but act otherwise
They go Lord, Your children, because You have asked
and we know Lord, the time is short
Your return is nigh
We go Lord, because of those that have not heard
because of those not ready
We go Lord, for the love of our brother
that You have given us.
We go Lord, because of Your love

Rebecca Stepp Revels

<u>I Will Rejoice</u>

I will rejoice Lord
singing Your name
shouting praises to the Heavens
as I dance
with You

I will rejoice Lord
in all things Yours
for Your master plan
covers all things
Yours

I will rejoice Lord
in the coming storms
for I know in them
I will find courage
in You

I will rejoice Lord
in the rains that fall
and the winds that blow
feeling Your strength
and peace

I will rejoice Lord
in the coming night
for I know in my heart
of the coming dawn
and You.

I will rejoice Lord
for I know in my heart
time is short
soon Sweet Lord, I'll see
You

Blessed

I Worry Lord

I worry Lord, about those that contort Your word
that take and twist it
turning it into something that it is not
making it say, what they wish
to fit their will, not Yours
I worry Lord, for those that change Your word
for in so doing, they cause others, to turn away
to run away, from You
not understanding that it is not Your word that is wrong
but the actions and manipulations of man
I worry Lord, for those that alter Your word, and its meaning
for Your word is pure and holy lasting into eternity and beyond
and man's but a vapor, here and then not
but its harm is every lasting
when it causes someone, to turn away
I worry Lord, for those that do this
have a grand and great audience
as they stand on the corners and on the hilltops
on the streets and in the shops
spouting their ways and condemnations
spewing their venom and their hatred
they distort Your word and Your ways
and those that do not understand, accept
that this is correct, not knowing the truth
but even You Lord, warned us to watch and be wary
for there would be those false prophets
yet the lost, do not understand and they see those
and they accept, and I worry
for those that turn away
and for those, that cause them, to close their ears
harden their hearts, and move closer into the everlasting pit.

Rebecca Stepp Revels

I ask You Lord, to give me voice
that I may stand on this mountaintop
stand on this street or in this shop
and in humble humility, share Your word
that I may, in quiet compassion

with gentle voice and touch
share as my Lord did
with all that will hear

I ask You Lord
to give me the heart, to see the eager
to find the lost and the ones in pain
and share Your word and Your ways

in truth as You meant it to be
not twisted or altered to fit my needs
I ask You Lord, to give me a wisdom
to discern what is right from wrong
what words of Yours that need be heard
explained, given as a light in the dark.
to the lost, to those that turn away
to the ones, that twist Your word
I ask Lord
for I worry

Blessed

Reach Out, Be a Light

Reach out
to the lonely, the afraid
be a light
shining in the darkness
so that they may see
Reach out
to the sick, the tired
be a light
so they will see their way to rest
Reach out
to those that hunger and thirst
be a light
so they may find their way to be fed
Reach out
to the less desirable among you
be a light
as I was a light to you.

The poor are always among us
poor not only in wealth
but in faith, for the wealth of the Lord's blessings
have not been poured upon them
it is not a wealth in material things
but a wealth in the peace and reassurances
of His magnificent love
a wealth in knowing His rest
when this life makes us weary
his comfort
when the strong winds of the storms blow
the wealth of knowing
above all things, His amazing and most comforting
grace.

Rebecca Stepp Revels

The wealth of knowing, some day we will be called home
and there will be pain no more.
Reach out
to those that are poor among you
be a light
so they may find their way.

~~~~~~~~~~~~~~~~~~

<u>I Believe</u>

I believe
that all those long years ago
You walked this earth
living as a man
so that we would know,
that You understand.
Born of a virgin
growing as a child
in wisdom and in strength
with a compassion of heart and touch
We would know
that You understand
temptation
You Understand
hunger and thirst
We would know
that You understand being tired
You walked this earth
healing the sick
feeding the hungry
suffering the pain
inflicted by man
bearing that cross
across a bleeding back

Blessed

knowing the worst was to come
blood flowed down stained cheeks
from a crown of thorns
shoved brutally down
nails driven, a cross lifted
as You hung there and died
death, horrible death
could not keep You
as You rose, having paid the price
walking this place fully God, fully man
rising up from the grave
Lamb of God, Perfect Savior
Sweet Lord

Gifts From You

Your light flowing down
guiding my path
leading me ever forward
showing me the way
to You

Your love flowing outward
covering me
granting to me peace
giving to me assurance
from You

Your Word spoken to my heart
giving to me a knowledge
a wisdom of Your way,
to lead me ever forward
to You

Rebecca Stepp Revels

Your forgiveness, a gift offered
freely for the acceptance
Your merciful grace,
unearned, undeserved, yet given
by You

Your gifts to me
Your gifts to all who believe
leading, comforting, teaching
all who reach out and accept, these precious gifts
from You

Your Love Overflows

There is a special feeling
that moves through my heart
bringing with it a loving peace
when I come to You Lord
in supplication, in reverence
I know Your presence
I feel You close to me
when I speak with You
it doesn't matter the topic
for Your love and concern, covers all
nothing is too trivial, nothing unimportant
when it is brought to You
for You are in control of everything
You know all, missing nothing
Knowing before it happens
understanding, what reactions are going to come
Letting me know, of Your presence
with that feeling of joy that can only be felt
when You move in my heart
Comforting me, in times of sadness
calming me, in times of distress
listening to me, when I speak to You, in prayerful supplication

Blessed

speaking to me, when I need Your word
showing me, when I need to see Your miracles
It is joy, immeasurable, unstoppable joy
that flows through my heart
a gift of Your Spirit, that moves within
I know, when You are close
Your voice, music to my heart
song to my soul
I am humbled by the glory of You
that shines around me
I am overwhelmed, by the feelings
falling trembling to my knees, unable to stand
as Your glory flows around me
showing me, reminding me
that You are always with me
always near, always listening
guiding me, to where You need me to be
instructing me, on what I need to do
to be used as a tool in Your hands
a worker in Your fields
I am overwhelmed by the feelings
of Your love, love that flows freely down
covering me, cleansing me, forgiving me
of all my sins and failings
My heart knows Your presence
My heart, knows Your love
I know, how unworthy I am, sinner that I am
yet still I know Lord
How You Love me
and my heart, is overwhelmed and overjoyed
as Your love over flows
spilling down, covering all that will receive and accept
the special feelings that are You
as Your love, over flows
filling my heart, bringing the tears of joy, laughter and love
that come, only
when Your love, over flows

Rebecca Stepp Revels

<u>Lord, I Believe</u>

I believe
That Your love is shared with a soft gentle voice
speaking words of kindness and love
spoken in a language to build up
to comfort the weak and the weary
to strengthen and encourage
those who feel as if they cannot go on
Words given in a sharing of wisdom
instructing with compassion those that hear,
so that they may in turn share, with compassion
with out condemnation

I believe
That Your love is shared with a tender touch
a gentle hand reaching out in compassion
one hand offered to another, no matter who they may be
one hand offered to another, to help them to their feet
to offer a friendship, to offer assistance, to offer love

I believe
That You are love, pure and holy
Your compassion for all encompasses all
a never ending love, wrapping Your children
in the comforting peace that is You
Mercy and peace given freely by Your grace
forgiveness for all, offered for the acceptance

I believe Lord, I believe

~~~~~~~~~~~~~~~~~~~~

Blessed

<u>In Faith</u>

In faith, I walk
trusting Lord, in Your words
believing, that time grows short
in faith, I walk
keeping my eyes to You
watching, for You Lord
in faith, I walk
sharing what I feel of You
sharing what You give to me
in faith, I walk
watching for the chance to give
hoping for the opportunity to share
In faith, I walk
listening always for Your voice
speaking to me, encouraging
giving to me a love, like none other
gifting me with a peace
that can come only Lord, from You

in faith, I walk
knowing, that soon Lord
with You,
I will know the pains of this place no more

in faith
I believe

Rebecca Stepp Revels

<u>Trust in You</u>

I will place in You Lord, all my trust
that as I walk this place
You will always be right here with me
by my side, in my heart
leading me, to the places I need to be
giving me the strength to get there
while doing the things, that you need for me to do
along the way
I trust Lord, that no matter what I meet
what problems that wait, causing me to stumble
You will be there, to lift me up
encouraging me, leading me from beside me, within me
along the way, should I grow weary, You will give me strength
You will and do see my tears, You know the things that cause me fear
for You Lord, are always here, so near
guiding me, through the labyrinth of this life
You are here Lord, sheltering me from the storm
while using the storm to teach me, to trust more
believe more, in You, being here, beside me
I trust You Lord, that You know my hunger
for things of You. Seeking Your wisdom as well as Your compassion
You will in Your time, teach me, show me the things I need to know
so that I will in turn be able to share with others
teach me, Your way, Your words so that as I grow in trust
I grow in knowledge, giving me the seeds of Your love to sow
in the fields of the lost and heartsick
I have all trust in You Lord
for I know, You have given to me a great gift
in Your love, in Your forgiveness, in the blessing Lord
of Trust.
In You Lord, I have full trust
in my heart I believe
that You love me

Blessed

<u>Hour of Your Arrival</u>

The hour comes Lord
I feel time grows short
even though the hour not known
that You will come,
to call Your children home
away from this place
away from this time of turmoil
to be with You
No more sorrow
no more pain in our heart
as our travels are through
we are home, with You
The hour comes Lord
even though no one knows the time
excitement begins to build
so all of Your children hurries
for the harvest in the field
we know Lord, we know
of Your all encompassing Love
so we hurry to tell all we find
so that none, will be left behind
I feel that time grows short Lord
show me what I must do
before the hour of Your arrival
when we go, to be with You.

Rebecca Stepp Revels

<u>What I Find in You Lord</u>

When I was lost, wandering alone
You found me
calling my name, speaking to me
offering to me, what could be found no where else
I heard Your voice, and I knew
I felt Your Spirit
moving in me, calling me
as understanding dawned
and I knew, I called upon You
answering Your knock on my heart
answering Your calling my name
and nothing, has been the same
for now, I never walk alone
I feel Your presence
always with me
calming the storms, comforting my fears
when the dark of the night, of the storms approach
You are my Light, You are The Light
shining through, showing the way
and my heart, knows Your joy
when my soul thirsts
You are the Living Water that quenches that thirst
when I hunger for more
You Lord, are the Bread of Life, Your word fills me
and satisfies my hunger for knowledge of You
I feel Your presence Lord
when I grow weary in this life and its struggles
I feel You, leading me to a place of rest
and my heart sings and my soul does dance
for there is no love, no peace
like the merciful redeeming grace
that I find, in You.

Blessed

Not Mere Words

Words,
they are not merely words
while they may be simple
easy to understand
words of love
peace, gentleness
words of compassion
knowing and acting that way
not mere words
but history and future
an explanation of the time beginning
an explanation of how it will end
not mere words
they are words, an expression of You
a promise from You
they are Your words
given to and written down by man
yet kept safe and alive
all this time
so that we will know You
and the things that You wish of us
promises made to us
not through mere words
but Your words
Your promise
Your love.

Rebecca Stepp Revels

The Bridegroom Comes

The morning comes
make ready
for as the morning comes
as does the Bridegroom
comes for His bride
make ready
for we are not forewarned
of the time
make ready
for He could come
any moment, any time
and call the names
of those in the Book
calling them to His table
make ready
watch the skies
as we wait His time
invite those you meet
invite those you know
tell them of He who comes
tell them of the Bridegroom
and of the need
to make ready.

Blessed

<u>No Greater Peace</u>

I know of no greater peace
no calm better, than what is in my heart
that has come from You
many winds of storm have blown
bringing rains that flood this life
with worry and fears
Your voice, comforts me
with but a word, calming the storms
filling my life with Your light
Your presence, takes me to a place of rest
where no storms may enter
as I build up my strength to better walk with You
When I tremble, whether from fear or exhaustion
You are there, wrapping Your love around me
comforting me, reassuring me of Your presence
and I know, no greater peace
than I know at that moment
moments with You
that I carry with me always, depending on
relying on, the knowledge of Your closeness to me
in my heart, I know peace
in my soul, I am at peace
knowing, You

Rebecca Stepp Revels

<u>The Words That Move Me</u>

To share
the feelings that are in my heart
express them to any and to all
that happen upon them
to share
what speaks to me
be it in whispers
a song
or a shout from the highest heavens
to share
what moves my spirit
and causes my heart to sing
hoping, that others that see
can feel it as well
an in the sharing
they too will sing
that their soul will dance
and then they too
share
until then
I share
the words
that move
me

Blessed

<u>Why Lord</u>

From their knees,
with clasped hands
and closed eyes
they ask,
Why am I here?
Why is it Lord,
that I am here?
You must have a reason for me
to be
After the things that have happened
I can not help but wonder
what are Your plans
for I know in my heart
that if there was not a reason
for me to be
I would have left this place long ago
Why is it Lord
that I am here
what is it You would have for me
to be
what task, would You have me do?
is there some grand and glorious thing
waiting for my arrival
is that the reason
for my survival
From their knees
hidden in corners
under bridges
out in the cold of the night
they wonder and they ask
why, am I here?
I have walked through the fires of abuse
and been a substance abuser
drowning my sorrow in drink
to forget, to survive

Rebecca Stepp Revels

to come out alive
Storms did not take me
shots that were fired, that missed
how Lord, at such close range
did an angel stand between
unseen?
Fights to stay alive
through hunger and thirst
loneliness and feelings of abandonment
and yet, I am here still
Disease came for me
of the heart, of the body, of the mind
unbidden, unexpected
but You held my hand
for You have a plan
and I wonder Lord
I hold no fear to hear
why, Lord
am I here?

~~~~~~~~~~~~~~~~~~~~~~~~~~~

<u>Many Walking</u>

There are many walking
that do not know You Lord
walking among us, living a life
without You, not understanding Your way
because they have not been told Your word

There are many longing
for something, someone
a longing that they do not understand
for they have not been told
that the heart yearns for You
so they seek blindly
oft times falling into the darkness
lost and stumbling, crying out

Blessed

from a desire they do not understand
because they have not been told

There are many walking
lost, caught in a hopelessness
that they know no end to
they can not see the Light waiting
they do not hear the Voice calling
they do not recognize it
they do not answer
they need, someone to tell them
to share with them Lord, Your Word and Your Way

You have said Lord,
that the fields are ready, but the workers few
send me Lord, to be a worker, for You
give to me the words
to share with those that are lost
the wisdom to explain, You
and how You have paid the cost

give to me the words
to explain, to show the way
to plant a seed of understanding
tell me, what to say

There are many walking
among us that do not know You Lord
help me, Lord, to share.

Rebecca Stepp Revels

<u>Faith in You</u>

Faith

To believe
without having seen

But dear Lord
how I have seen You
in the early morning dawn
in the last evening rays of the sun
walking alone with You
along paths long or short
in the flowers that grow
giving beauty and color to this land
and food to the creatures created by Your hand
I have seen You Lord
in the rushing waters of the river
in the stillness of the lake
in the clouds drifting slowly past
I have seen You Lord
in the endless blue sky
or the palette of autumn leaves
Watching the flight of the bird
or butterfly, go by
I have seen You
in this place that You have created
and I believe
and my faith is strong
for I hear Your voice
call my name
I feel Your presence
in my heart
and I know, I believe
because I have seen
daily Lord, grows
my faith.

Blessed

<u>Glory to the Father</u>

The pain Lord
that You endured for me
suffering, bleeding
hanging from a tree
but for all that is done
a price must be paid
You said You would
the decision made
coming here
with no greater love
than to show the world
glory to the Father above

<u>All Things</u>

When the worries of this life come
I turn to You Lord
giving them all to You
asking You to calm my seas of stress
still the winds of worry
bring a calm harbor to my heart
that can come
will come
only from You Lord
giving me peace and assurance
that with You
all things are well.

Rebecca Stepp Revels

<u>Did You Notice</u>

How bright
did the sun shine Lord
when You walked this sod?
Did You stand on a hill
watching the sun rise over the horizon?
Did you stand on the shore of the lake
watching as it reflected off the water?
hearing children laugh and play
as parents kept watchful eye?
Did You stand Lord
seeing the dust as it blew across the road You walked
coating Your sandals with each step.
Did You notice as You walked?

The people calling out to You
begging for just a touch of Your hand
to be able to touch, just the hem of Your garment
so that healed, they could dance in Your shadow
as they follow You
shouting praises as they go
understanding, believing, You were not mere man
not just a prophet passing
they understood, You were so very much more.
Did You notice?

Today Lord, in faith, many so many call Your name
reaching to You, seeking You
needing to hear Your voice, feel Your presence close
walking along the road with them
traveling this sod once again in their heart
reaching out, hoping for that touch
desiring, to touch the hem of Your garment
so that with joyous abandon they may dance in Your shadow.

I know Lord, that You see

Blessed

I know Lord, that You hear each cry and call
that You do, indeed notice
each of Your children in their times of sorrow
I know You see, and in seeing, reach out
with a healing, calming touch

bringing peace and reassurance of Your presence
in a place that can be so difficult to walk
as the dust coats our sandals Lord
help us to stand on the shores of the lake

seeing the light reflecting off the water
and know Your love, reflecting off the seas of distress
that is this life
and know in our heart, that You do see
and with a touch, heal our heart of the pain
calm our souls of the worries
until the day, we are with You
and this journey, is no more.

~~~~~~~~~~~~~~~~~~

Grant to me Lord

Touch my heart oh Lord
grant me the peace
that comes from You
for this day that I face
and the tomorrows that wait
grant me Lord
the assurance and reassurance
that You are here, walking with me

Rebecca Stepp Revels

along this road
give to me the knowledge of You
that I desire, that I may share
grant me Lord, Your love
in an abundance that overflows
and shows, to all around me
so that they too will be touched
feeling Your presence and mercy
grant me Lord, this day
the things that will help me through
and I can shout to all Lord
the glories of You.

~~~~~~~~~~~~~~~~

Hope

The world dear Lord
is in so much turmoil
Wars spread like disease
infecting and effecting all that it touches
and war, touches all
famines Lord, stretch endless
as many go hungry, reaching out a trembling hand
a frail body weak and tired
hunger dear Lord,
touches us all
storms rise up bringing great winds
tearing apart all that they reach
destroying all in its path
tearing away lives
bringing with it fear and worries
bringing harm and danger
and touching us all
rains fall, causing rivers to rise
flooding the lands and towns

Blessed

pushing parts of lives before the rampage
washing away things
taking away people
leaving destruction in its wake
touching us all
leaving no one

in my heart Lord
rests the hope in You
knowing that You see all things
having not abandoned us to the destruction
that You wait Lord
ever at the ready
for us to call on You
Waiting patiently for us
to return to You
promising that should we do this
our lands will be healed

in my heart Lord I know
that the time here grows short
the things of which we were told

are falling into place
preparing for Your return
in my heart Lord I know
I hear You whispering to me

I feel in my heart Your love
so I share the words
and I hope
that seeds are planted
causing hope and belief to grow
in the hearts of those that read.

Rebecca Stepp Revels

<u>Draw me Closer Lord</u>

draw me closer Lord
into Your love
allow me to feel it
flowing over me
bringing a gentle peace
calming my heart and soul
washing me clean of my iniquity

draw me Lord
closer to You every moment
of every day
walking with You
talking with You Lord
hearing Your voice
speaking to my heart
allowing me to know You
as Lord, as Savior, as friend

draw me closer Lord
in this walk with You
fill me with Your Spirit
allow me to recognize
Your merciful grace and love
the redemption that is from You
the forgiveness that is You
fill me Lord, with Your love

draw me closer Lord, to You
in every situation, every conflict
allow me to hear Your voice
feel Your presence near
bringing to me, Your understanding
granting to me, Your peace
so that I too, am able to forgive

Blessed

just as You forgive

draw me closer Lord
closer to You

~~~~~~~~~~~~~~~~~~~

<u>Just One Day</u>

Just one day Lord
for just this one day
allow me to see
those along the way
that are in need of You
those that are hurting
lonely and sad
those that are tired
lost
allow me Lord
to see them as I walk
give me the compassion
to reach out to them
offering what I have
that may in the ways they need
help them
a helping hand
a loving hand
the hand, of a friend

Rebecca Stepp Revels

just one day Lord
allow me to hear the cries
of those around me
that are seeking, something
someone
that can help them in their hour of need
that can hear them call
and will reach out to them
offering what they need
just this one day Lord
let me know the things
that I need, to give to those
that need
seeing them, hearing them
as You would
offering, giving, to them
as You would
then Lord, I ask of You
for just one more day
at a time
opening my eyes more
opening my ears
opening my heart
just one day
at a time.

Straight to You

When the storm clouds seem their darkest
bringing the heavy rains that threaten
winds that tear at all
in the midst of the darkness
I see Your light, shining out, guiding me
straight to You
lighting the path before me

Blessed

so that my steps remain true
straight to You
with a word, You still the winds
calming the fears they bring
bringing peace to a worried heart
and rest to a weary soul
as You guide me to safe haven
straight to You
When the storm clouds seem their darkest
hope within begins to dim
I hear Your voice speaking
calling me from the rains
into the blessed peace that is You
calling me, guiding me
straight to You.

Tears Fall

tears fall
streaming down a face
broken

hands reach
seeking assistance
broken

hearts search
for something unknown
lost

tears fall
streaming down a face
overjoyed

Rebecca Stepp Revels

hands raised
towards the Heavens
toward You

hearts sing
overjoyed with praise
found

~~~~~~~~~~~~~~~~~~~~~~

<u>Asking Lord</u>

Hello Lord,
I'm here, asking of You a favor
give me Your strength
to make it through this day
the evil one Lord, knows my weakness
and uses them often against me
catching me at my most vulnerable
so I struggle against what I know is wrong
attempting to stand in Your Light
doing what is right
I ask Lord, for Your strength,
to be able to stand more strong
giving You, this struggle, giving you this fight
I am asking Lord
for Your peace, so that when the darkness comes
creeping and sneaking around
doing its best to bring me down
I can easily turn away, and turn to You

Blessed

standing in Your peace and comfort
worrying not, as You have control of all
I am asking Lord
for my weaknesses are many
and I do so easily fall, when I try to stand alone
stand Lord, with me
give me Your strength and peace
take my worries and stress
let me learn from them, but not fall to them
bless me Lord with Your light
bless me Lord with Your peace
and give me Lord
the strength to stand strong
reflecting You, in all I do.
Thank you dear Lord, once again.

No Matter

no matter
the winds that blow

no matter
the rain that falls

no matter
how dark the clouds

Your light
shines through

no matter
how hot or how cold

no matter

Rebecca Stepp Revels

the time

no matter
all of these earthly things

Your light, Your love
shines through

no matter
how far I go

no matter
the mistakes I make

no matter
how I may fail

Your light
shines through

and I know
peace

~~~~~~~~~~~~~~~~~~~

Shouting Praises

shouting Your praises Lord
are we all, shouting them out loud
standing along the path that You trod
walking along the road we travel
shouting and singing, praises to You.
Reaching for the hem of Your garment
seeking where Your shadow will fall
shouting out Your praises

Blessed

to be heard, by one and all
are we clinging to what You offer
coveting Your love
shouting out Your praises
for the forgiveness that You give
blessed peace and comfort
assurance of redemption
no matter how low we've fallen
or how often
as we come back to You
reaching for Your garment
seeking out Your love
shouting from the mountaintops
how great, how great thou art

Such is Your Love

As the rain falls gently down
refreshing the earth
giving drink to the life below
such is Your love

The sun hung in the daytime sky
shining down onto this place
bringing warmth, bringing light
such, is Your love

The darkness of night
covering this place in its time
wrapping us in a time of rest
such, is Your love

As the fruit of the tree, and seed of the ground grows

Rebecca Stepp Revels

feeding those of this place
nourishing the body
such, is Your love

You came to this place
to hang on a tree, Your blood flowing down
paying the price no one else could pay
such is Your love

An offering of redemption
merciful grace unmeasured
forgiveness of all things
such, is Your love

~~~~~~~~~~~~~~~~~~

Over Things Seen

Dear Lord
Through these eyes
I have seen many things
some of which have caused pain
the intentional abuse of the weak
those that ignore the needs
of the poor or the lost
those that are doing without
as they watch the many that have
turn their head away
tears have flowed
coursing down cheeks

Blessed

empathy, for the suffering

great beauty has filled my vision
in the form of rainbows and rain drops
flowers that dance from the weight
of bees and butterflies
water splashing over obstacles in its path
sending a spray up to cool the passerby
the look of joy on the face of a child
sheer pleasure in the look of the aged
as they receive a hug from a friend
tears have flowed
coursing down cheeks
out of joy of the happiness

many things
have these eyes seen
overjoyed and with great excitement
over the good
refusing
to close over the sadness
from the ugliness
that comes with this life

tears have flowed
tears will flow
coursing down cheeks
over things seen.

Rebecca Stepp Revels

I Hear You

In the stillness, I hear Your voice
speaking to me
guiding me through this journey
bringing me to You
encouraging me, in the things You wish
In the stillness I hear You
and I am at peace
In the mad rush of things
when worries and stress are high
fear of the things in the darkness
I hear Your voice, calling to me
the shining light of Your words
guide me through, to You
and I am at peace
In all things, that are
the clear bright shining moments
the dark and stormy times
I hear Your voice, calling to me
encouraging me, along the way
guiding and encouraging, giving me strength
to make my way, to You

Blessed

<u>Worshiping You Lord</u>

A song on my lips, sang just for You
the words straight from my heart
sang by my soul, to You
as I stand in the light of Your glory
under the shining mercy of Your loving grace
I worship You Lord, I sing songs of love to You
for all that You have done for me, always
as You walk with me, stand with me
along this journey of life
showing me what I need know
showing me the beauty of this place
understanding, holding me when I cry over the suffering
strengthening me, to reach of for those in need
A song Lord, in my heart, a song, of worship for You
as I stand here, feeling Your presence, feeling Your love
knowing just how real You are
knowing, that You have a deep abiding love for me
I dance Lord, to the music that is Your word
the melody that is Your peace
singing Lord, a song of worship for You
each moment of my day, Loving You Lord
in thanks for Your love for me
gracing me Lord, blessing me with Your mercy
blessing me, with Your forgiveness
a song of worship Lord, in my heart
a song of worship, sang by my soul
harmonizing with Your Holy Spirit
sang Lord, just for You.

Rebecca Stepp Revels

<u>How Many</u>

Time here in this place
grows ever shorter
soon Lord, I know
it will be time
for Your return
How many Lord
are ready?
How many, look for You?
do they understand
that time grows short?
Are those that know Lord
sharing You? Sharing the news of Your coming
Prepared and preparing others for that day
do they look to the sky in anticipation
wondering, is today the day
seeking, to see Your face
understanding, how short is the time
How many Lord, are ready
looking for You
in joyful anticipation
excitement of that day growing
having a heart that trembles
waiting, for You
sharing Your word, sharing You
with all that will hear
blessing others, with the blessing of You
explaining, sharing, Your merciful grace
telling, of the greatest gift
the most wonderful act of love
the price that You paid
for the redemption of man
forgiveness, straight from You
How many Lord
are ready?
How many

Blessed

look to the sky
in joyful anticipation
of You
knowing
that time is short.

<u>You See Me</u>

You see Lord
when I walk within reach of temptation
You hear, as it teases me
calls to me
offers the easy way
You see me Lord
as I struggle against the dark
as I fight against what whispers my name
calling to me from the side of the road I walk
You see me Lord
in my weakness
when I slip and fall
allowing a word, or a feeling that is not Yours
You understand Lord
when I cry over my actions
when my heart aches in the knowledge of my wrongs
You understand, my regrets
You see me Lord
when I go down to my knees
asking You Lord, for forgiveness
for all those things
You see me
asking for strength to walk
staying in Your light
staying in Your peace
You see me Lord
in all of these things

Rebecca Stepp Revels

    moving closer to You
        Lord,
    in all of these things
        I see You
  moving ever closer, to me.

~~~~~~~~~~~~~~~~~~~~

<u>Never Alone</u>

In my darkest hour, when in my sadness I felt so alone
You were with me, never having left me
seeing the things I endured
because of the road I had taken
hearing my cries, as the storm rose higher
the winds of pain blew stronger
I stood lost and seemingly alone in the dark
bearing the brunt of the storm
for it was I that had walked away
It was I, that allowed the winds to blow me off course
and it was I, that suffered
In my darkest hour, when I felt the most afraid
You called to me, knowing You alone could bring me out of the pit
In my darkest hour, as the storms gathered strength against me
I looked and I saw You, reaching out to me
calling to me, to come back to You

In my brightest hour, I looked to the dawn
in an ever brightening sky, where the winds were at peace
the rains had ceased to fall upon me
in my brightest hour, when I was once again back safely with You
walking Lord, with You, the suffering was gone
my soul sang its praises to You
as my heart danced in the joy Lord, that is You
for I knew, that when I was in my darkest hour
You had never left me, and I was never alone.

~~~~~~~~~~~~~~~~~~~~

Blessed

<u>No One Lord</u>

No one Lord, can do the things, You do
There is no one Lord,
that can do, the things, that You have done
So many with hardened heart, misunderstand
turning a deaf ear, to Your voice
refusing to hear Your Word
when Your word Lord, is a message of Love
It is our guidelines for this life
meant to teach peace and joy
Your word Lord, tells us, of You
The life that You lived, and how in turn
we should live ours.
You came Lord, to pay the price
that no one else could pay
and in that payment, brought grace to us all
You stand waiting Lord, for us
holding out, to us, Your nail scarred hands
scars from that crown of thorns upon Your brow
but in Your eyes, the look of loving forgiveness
no one Lord, could do, what You did
no one Lord, could offer, what You do
no one Lord, can wash my sins away
forgiving me fully for all things
giving to me, life eternal with You
no one Lord, can do, what You do

Rebecca Stepp Revels

<u>Walk This Place</u>

I will walk this place
in the peace You give
understanding, it is hard to hold
for temptations wait
reaching out for me at every turn
hiding in the dark, waiting
for my passing
teasing me, with the simplicity
of slipping
I will walk this place
in the knowledge and assurance
that You are with me
You will guide my steps
as long as I look to You
accepting Your guidance
following Your light to my next step
hearing Your voice
instead of the calls of temptation
I will walk this place
seeking the lost, the poor, the lonely and afraid
with Your grace and merciful wisdom
so as to share with them
what I have found in You
I ask You Lord
that as I do walk this place
I never forget, never step away from the feeling
that is You, walking here, beside me

Blessed

<u>You Are With Me</u>

I saw the storm clouds rising
knowing what was to come
yet I feared not the winds
because You Lord are by my side

I saw the lightning flash
tearing bright slashes across the sky
but I feared not the lightning
for You were with me

I heard the thunder rumbling
shaking the ground on which I stood
yet in the thunder I felt no fear
for You stood with me

I felt the rains begin to fall
hard and fast and strong
still in this, I felt no fear
for You, sheltered me

I saw the storm approaching
felt it as it began
but there was no fear
as You Lord, sheltered me leading me through

I saw the storm approach
but as I stood in trust and faith with you
when the winds were stilled
From the shelter of Your arms, I saw the rainbow.

Rebecca Stepp Revels

I Willingly Walk

I will walk this place
in the peace You give
understanding, it is hard to hold
for temptations wait
reaching out for me at every turn
hiding in the dark, waiting
for my passing
teasing me, with the simplicity
of slipping
I will walk this place
in the knowledge and assurance
that You are with me
You will guide my steps
as long as I look to You
accepting Your guidance
following Your light to my next step
hearing Your voice
instead of the calls of temptation
I will walk this place
seeking the lost, the poor, the lonely and afraid
with Your grace and merciful wisdom
so as to share with them
what I have found in You
I ask You Lord
that as I do walk this place
I never forget, never step away from the feeling
that is You, walking here, beside me

Blessed

<u>Safe In You</u>

Lord help us as we stand here
our back to the wall
helpless in the face
of things we can not change
frightened, at what may come from this
worried, that we know not how to deal with what is to come
take this from me Lord
take my worries and fears
hide them away forever in You.
As the darkness closes in
and the night grows ever colder
wrap me in Your protection
secure me in Your arms
so that fear can not last
worries can not reach me
I am with You
safe in You
Protect me Lord
calm me I ask, in the face of things I fear
yet do not know
comfort me, with Your loving grace
so that I fear nothing
as there is nothing to fear
I ask this Lord, in humble supplication
not only for me dear Lord
but for all Your children
for all of those that look to You
trusting in You
but yet, have these moments of weakness and fear
reach out to us Lord,
take us I ask, into the safety and comfort of Your love
give us the peace
that can only come from You
Our Lord, Our Rock, Our Salvation

Rebecca Stepp Revels

<u>Break Me Lord, of Self</u>

Bring me to my knees Lord
before You
break me from myself
heal me, complete me, for You
break me, of my pride
the assurance that I can do it
on my own
bring me to You
closer to You
every day that I walk
bring me closer
so that I may feel You
moving in me
living, residing, in my heart
freeing me, from the ills of this life
healing me, from its pain
bring me, Lord, to my knees
before You
break me, from myself
allow me Lord, to feel Your power
moving, in me, through me
give to me, what I need
the words, the compassion
that is Yours
so that I may share
so that I may plant a seed for You
where ever, and every where
that I go
break me Lord of self
heal me Lord
I humbly ask
in You

Blessed

<u>Always</u>

Struggling alone this way
feet dragging from exhaustion
eyes barely open
as I tremble, so tired
my mind fights for coherent thought
but none comes
words mix and mingle making no sense
and the darkness knows
sending out the offers. the temptations
hoping in my tired mind, I will relent
but as I stumble and fall
I reach out to You Lord
and You catch my hand
lifting me up from the dust
holding me safely in Your arms
as You guide my steps
to a place of rest
A place, where my weary body can relax in peace
where I can regain my strength
safely in You
hearing Your voice offering words of quiet comfort
feeling Your presence guarding over me while I sleep
knowing that You will always be here
watching over me
guiding me
in all things
loving me
When my strength is renewed
and I can continue on this walk
You will be with me, ever mindful
of how I am
You will be with me
offering the peace and strength
that You know I need

Rebecca Stepp Revels

to walk this walk
to fight the offers of temptations
to continue to do the works
that You have given me
and as I walk
You will be with me
guiding, comforting, loving
always

~~~~~~~~~~~~~~~~~~~~~~~~~~~~

<u>Into the Storm</u>

I will walk
knowing
that You are here
with me
strengthening me
guiding me
to Your light
and Your refuge
Into the storm
I will run
thanking You Lord
that I am worthy of this
a way, to grow my faith
to make me strong, in You
Into the storm
I will dance
singing songs of praise
for I know
You are here
You will never leave me
no matter how dark the way
I will walk.

~~~~~~~~~~~~~~~~~~~~~~~~~~~~

Blessed

<u>Faithfully</u>
We are given the choice
to believe, or not
we can look to the skies
shake our fists at the storms
turn away and deny
seal our fate
we are given the chance
to look to the dawn
see a new light
bringing new life
a chance at wonderful things
a future that waits our decision
we are given the ability
to say yes, I believe
finding that belief
in faith alone
trusting in the Words written in red
to change us, allowing us, bringing us
to a position
where we are more like You, Lord
we are given the chance
to make a choice
based on faith
the voice calling out to our hearts
offering merciful grace and forgiveness
offering redemption from our failings
if we but reach out
accepting the offering
taking the chance
by making the choice
and stepping out
in faith.

Rebecca Stepp Revels

<u>My Faith is my Song</u>

You are the song in my heart
as I sing my praises to You Lord
the words come easily
for my joy in You is real
my faith in You is strong
which is my song

You are the music in my heart
giving my soul cause to dance
as the notes come easily
as the tune plays on
because of a faith that is strong
playing praises Lord, to You

You are the reason in my heart
that I smile as I walk this life
my steps light, yet sure
because it is Your voice I hear
calling me home, where I belong
my faith is my song
singing praises Lord, to You

Blessed

<u>Never Alone, When Walking With You</u>

the road is long
winding
turning
this way
turning
that way
through deep valleys
over steep hills
along rivers
and desert sands
along the way
are stumbling blocks
along the way
are easy times
the road
of life
travels through
times of beautiful sunlight
soft moonlight
there are moments
of rain and storms
floods of fear and stress
along this road
friends will walk by our side
or we will at times
walk alone
but never alone
when we walk
with You Lord.

Where Ever

I can make it through
what ever comes
as long
as I keep my eyes to You
no matter the night
and how dark it becomes
all will be well
while I stay in Your light
I will not fear
the winds that blow
the rains that fall
as long as You are near
for Your truth I know
that no matter the storm
no matter what worries come
You are with me where ever I go

Blessed

<u>For Them I Fear</u>

Not the dark
nor what lurks there
with yellow eyes
from under the bed do stare
no fear
not of heights
so far above the ground
up higher than anything
no safety net to be found
no fear
not of snakes
nor things that crawl and creep
over none of these
will I lose sleep
no fear
not the dogs that growl
nor the cats that hiss
I do not worry
over any of this
no fear
the only fear
I hold in my mind
is for those that don't hear
and are left behind
fear for them
and what awaits
just inside
of hell's broad gates
misery and pain
confusion now clear
eternal damnation
its for them, I fear.

Rebecca Stepp Revels

Sweet Peace

Peace, sweet peace
flowing through my heart
giving rest from the storm
that is the day I must pass through
peace, in the sound of Your voice
speaking to my heart
whispering to my soul
causing them to sing out in praise
to dance in the joy of Your love
peace, in the sight of You
and the gifts You have blessed us with
here in this place
bringing happiness in the appreciation
peace, sweet peace
that flows through my life
because You are a part of me
I am a part of You
finding You in everything, every where
walking with me
guiding me forward
as I walk in Your light
seeing You in this place
hearing You, in my heart
feeling Your touch on my life
giving to me
sweet peace

Blessed

<u>I Heard You Call My Name</u>

When I was lost,
wandering about this place
without You
When the darkness was what I knew
not You
struggling to find the way
through the pain
sinking into a deep pit of despair
wishing for better
needing more
not knowing where to go
where to look
as the darkness grew deeper
and the road stretched long before me
voices whispered from the hidden places
taunting, teasing, inviting me
to stray away, into the night
fear became a constant companion
weary was my walk
I heard Your voice, call my name
saying to me, "I am here"
at the sound my heart jumped in joy
knowing, understanding, feeling
what a jaded mind could not
I heard Your voice, call my name
as I felt Your presence close
reaching out to me
fear etched across my face
to trust someone new
but the peace that flowed
reaching out, wrapping around me
offering sweet rest
I heard Your voice, call my name

Rebecca Stepp Revels

inviting me, away from the pain
and as I reached out, to You
Your light began to shine
in a heart empty and dark
Your song of love filled me
Your lyrics of peace I learned
as my heart renewed,
danced with joyous abandon
bathed in Your forgiveness
wrapped in Your mercy and grace
Your light, leading my way
which was now not so long, nor lonely
for I was not alone
held safely, in Your arms of love.

~~~~~~~~~~~~~~~~~~~~~~~~~

When This World Strikes Out

When this world strikes out
inflicting a wounding blow
and the pain surrounds
like a storm approaching
winds whipping cruelly about
darkness like a cancer covers
bringing a fear that leaves one helpless
cringing in a corner, hiding
from the pain
hiding, from the fear
when this world, strikes out
laying claim to the innocent
bringing harm and confusion
as they wander helpless
seeking a way, seeking a friend
seeking someone, that will help
to find a way

Blessed

walking sidewalks among the crowds
yet so alone, as the crowds do not even see
the empty eyes, the eyes, filled
with pain, with hunger for something better
hiding in back alleys
hiding from fear in the cardboard box
seeking security under a bridge
hearing the storm blow around them
when this world strikes out
and a child cries
from the attack from one trusted
from the hunger of body, spirit or soul
as they hide in corners, or closets dark
crying silently
trembling in fear
hoping for a way out
hoping for someone to come

When this world strikes out
You see

You weep for Your lambs
and their pain
feelings that You understand
You weep
as You reach out to them
through miracles
through the work of Your children

You see and You weep
and You reach out to them
offering peace, security
a place of rest
out of the storm.

Rebecca Stepp Revels

<u>I Wonder</u>

Seeing the beauty
that is this place
gifts that You have given
I wonder
how will Heaven be
beauty beyond comprehension
peace beyond measure
the colors of love
flowing freely
If I stand on the mountain top
and look out across the land
seeing Your creation
how prefect it all is
I am in awe
and then I wonder
how much more so
Heaven will be
Endless blue skies
grace this place
green and golden fields stretch wide
trees, dressed in green
adorned in colors for fall
flowers dance happily in the breeze
as quiet water reflects
the gifts given by You
I look at all of this
and I wonder

Blessed

<u>In All Things</u>

with the morning sun that rises
even as it sets when evening comes
as the moon climbs high into the sky
and the stars glitter in the black velvet night

as the rains fall, refreshing, washing the earth
when the sun shines down, warming and drying
a soft wind blows, causing the leaves to sway
to the moments that all is still, all is quiet

with the tears of those that suffer
in the laughter of those at peace
in the silence of an empty heart
You are there

In all things, You are with us
every moment, You feel our pain,
our joy
we are never alone
as long as we are with You
for You have promised
that You will never leave or forsake us
in this
I thank you Lord

Rebecca Stepp Revels

One Comes

Alone on the street
afraid and hiding
in a corner, in a box
in an abandoned doorway
shrinking down
should someone look their way
alone and afraid
seeking
an answer to questions unasked
reasons, for things not understood
a hand, reaching out in aid

Alone in a city of tents
hungry and cold
fighting to survive
sitting on a fallen log, staring
at anything and at nothing
longing for a meal
a blanket to fight the cold
seeking answers
to questions not asked
reasons, for things not understood
a hand, reaching out in compassion

Alone in a sea of strangers
yet one, brings a word
of compassion and peace
offers a way, to find mercy
one comes, with a meal
to fight the hunger of the body
a blanket, to warm the body from the cold

Blessed

one comes, with words of peace
a compassionate hand
a loving heart
one comes
bringing words and actions
of the Savior.

In Compassion and Love

We are not here in this place
to pass judgment
that is not our calling
we are not here, on this walk
to condemn
it is not our place

We are here on this journey
passing through to our eternal home
to reach out to others
to act in compassion and love
to the weaker and lesser among us
to offer bread to the hungry
as the Lord fed the thousands
to offer drink to the thirsty
as the Lord did at the well
we are here,
to do all we can to bring aid to the suffering
peace to those afraid
knowledge
to those that do not understand
to walk as our Lord
acting in compassion
and love.

Rebecca Stepp Revels

A Compassionate Word

I hear You Lord, speaking to me
calling to me, feed my sheep
my heart aches for those
wandering, walking about this place
that haven't heard
or have heard, and do not understand
My heart weeps, for those that take Your word
and change it for their means
for they do much harm to the innocent
I hear You Lord, whispering to me
feed my lambs, and I look to the children
laughing in their innocence
while others, look out through empty eyes
afraid, alone, hurting from many pains
and I ache for them while my heart cries
and I ask You Lord,
I am one of meager means
how can I feed so many
in my heart, Your word moves
show them me, in your actions
reach out a gentle hand of compassion
speak a soft word of love
lay a hand of peace on the shoulder of the weary
speak to them of Me
share what You know in your heart
plant a seed, tend it lovingly
with mercy and love
feed my sheep
I feel You moving in my heart, calling to me
and my heart weeps for those
that do not know, that do not understand
and I wrap the love of the Lord around me
I hold on to the peace I have found

Blessed

taking His merciful grace as the blessing it is
and I look to the fields, and I see the harvest
I look to You Lord, I feel You close, waiting

Go with me Lord, guide me along this way
I feel Your smile, and hear You
'always, until the end of the age'
and I walk, with a gentle hand

I walk, with a compassionate word.
and I look to You Lord.

~~~~~~~~~~~~~~~~~~~~~~~~~~~

<u>So Great Is Your Love</u>

Do You weep Lord
over Your children
those that do not understand?
the ones that have not heard?
as they go about the days
living as only they know how
not knowing, for not having heard?
for those that have heard
and yet, turn away
for what ever reason in their heart
do You weep Lord, over them?
Reach out Your hand to them
as they walk away?
Do You weep Lord
over those that take Your word
and change it, manipulate it for their means?
do You weep, for those that it harms
causing them to turn away
for they can not see You, in this?

Rebecca Stepp Revels

Do You weep Lord, for those alone
on the streets, in homes, in crowds that do not see
for those that suffer, sickness, pain, abuse
do You hold out open arms
welcoming them to You, even though they do not see
Do You weep Lord, over one of Your children
that turns away, falls into the temptation of the darkness
walking away from the narrow road
onto the broad way of the lost
Does Your heart break Lord
as You look out upon this place
seeing the harvest ready, yet the workers so few
do You weep Lord?
I know You do
I know Lord, that You do.
Reach out, in gentle loving compassion
for those lost
reach out, with open arms, inviting all
seeking all, to come to You
I know Lord, that You weep
for so great, is Your love.

All Along

I have walked in the darkness
alone and afraid
seeing the evil there
feeling the emptiness
and how cold and unfeeling
it can be.
I have walked in the darkness
crawling in the ditches
hiding away from things unseen
crying over how far
just how far
I had fallen

Blessed

I have walked in the darkness
thinking all was lost
I was lost
wondering, seeking rescue
seeking, something else
as I crawled along the bottom
I have walked
on the dark side
with tears flowing
fears growing
despair soaked in the knowing
only the dark, rain soaked storms
I have been lost in the darkness
down on my knees, torn and bleeding

hope all gone
when I heard Your voice
calling to me, seeking me in the dark
reaching out to me, You brought me back to You
out of the darkening storms
out of the cold of despair
into the warmth of Your light
into the assurance of Your love
I heard Your voice, call my name
Your love wrapping around me
calming my fears, drying my tears
bringing me to Your peace

I heard Your voice calling to me
the compassion undeniable
as I stepped from the darkness
back into the light of hope
realizing, I had never been alone
You had stayed with me
watching over me, protecting me

Rebecca Stepp Revels

waiting, for me to realize
how far I had wandered
and how badly, I wanted back
waited, for me
to reach out to You
as You had been reaching out to me
all along.

<u>Hope Rests In You</u>

I see the storm clouds
growing on the horizon
looming large in the distance
as they move this way
I feel the winds as they pick up
blowing the dust around before it
stinging like a thousand needles
on the unprotected face
bringing tears to the eyes
yet I stand strong in You
my hope rests in Your Lord
as the rains come
falling pounding down
filling streams and rivers
threatening to flood
washing away, all that is not secure
I have built my house on Your Lord
You are the rock on which I stand
my hope, rests in You
as the thunder rumbles
shaking the ground
as the storms grow stronger
lightning tearing apart the skies

Blessed

I stand in assurance
I hold no fear
for all my hope, all my faith
rests in You Lord
and I will stand in this place
I will walk this way
knowing that no matter what comes
You are with me
You are my strength and my rock
and on me, this place has no hold
for You have surrounded me
with Your hedge of protection
I am wrapped securely in Your love
I will not worry or fear
for it is You Lord
that is my hope
in You Lord
is my eternity .

~~~~~~~~~~~~~~~~

Holding on to the Faith

Holding onto trust Lord
believing in You
Holding onto faith Lord
knowing You are true
as I travel, making my way
through this place
with my eyes toward heaven
and seeing Your face
feeling Your presence
always by my side
guiding the way
until with You, I'll abide
holding onto trust
in these things that I feel
holding on to faith

Rebecca Stepp Revels

that You are real
no matter what the others
may believe or say
I'm holding on to faith
that You are the Way
that You are always close
walking with me
from all my transgressions
I have been set free
holding on to faith
in You my King
looking forward to the day
when with the angels I'll sing
words of praise and glory
a beautiful song
one which I look forward to singing
for all eternity long
holding on to faith
that I have in You
holding on to the belief
Your words are true
holding on to the faith
as I journey through this way
holding on to the belief
I'll be with You, some day.

Blessed

Hope In The Answered Call

a gentle touch to the heart
a heart that is wounded and weary
lost in the sadness of this place
crying out, from the hopeless feelings
seeking answers to questions too many
seeking hope, when none can be found
a gentle touch, a compassionate word
sparks a light, before long dark
eyes turn to the light, seeking the way
taking the first step, toward peace
sweet peace long thought lost
a shore of rest, waiting
for the lost to find their way
a voice, calling out softly
bringing the lonely home
a healing to the wounded heart
a rest, to the weary soul
in the arms, of a loving Savior
waiting, open and inviting
to those that will but hear
for those that will but answer the call.

Rebecca Stepp Revels

<u>God Can</u>

At the time
When things seem most desperate
darkness surrounds
sadness abounds
and the pit of despair
has no bottom
when it seems as if there is no one
that can help
when all is lost
and there is no way to go on
God can

At the time
When the winds of the storms blow
rain pours down
pounds the ground
as the flood waters rise
lightning rends the sky
as the floods of hopelessness raise
you feel about to drown
in this sea of confusion
looking for a hand
seeing no one that is able to assist
God can

At the time
When hunger assails
the body is weak
nourishment you seek

Blessed

for more than just food
wandering lost, wondering
is there not something more
answers to questions
assurance of a better way
when no one can answer you
give you the reassurance of what you seek
God can

At the time
when you wander alone
avoiding the eyes of those you meet
in a business, in a home, on the street
confused and afraid

with a heart that trembles
and a soul that weeps
when no one can come to your aid
offer you a way out
as they hurry past, eyes avoided
fearing being too close
when you feel no one can help
you rise out of this pit of darkness
God can.

Raise your eyes to Him
His light
can guide you home
raise your eyes to Him
his love
will surround you
comfort you
reassure you
in a way that no one else can
but
God can.

With Us

There is a gentle feeling
when You are here
the storms calm
the clouds break away
allowing Your light
to shine through
a comfort to all
when storms come
knowing You are here
always and forever
reaching out to all
that are in need
using miracles
using those that believe
to reach out in compassion
to reach out in peace
to lift up the fallen
downtrodden, lost
showing the love
that is You
when storms come
there is a peace
in knowing
in believing without seeing
in seeing, when we open our eyes
and our hearts
that You are always and forever
with us

Blessed

<u>Finding You</u>

Looking for You Lord
finding You
in all things

the warmth of the sun
the cool of the breeze
the laughter of a dancing brook

Looking for You Lord
as I journey
finding You easily
in all things

the colors of the flowers
swaying in the fields
filled with butterflies and bees

I look for You Lord
as I travel
opening my eyes
and my heart
finding You, in all things

the laughter of children
the hug of a friend
the touch of compassion from a stranger

I look for You Lord
as I go

Rebecca Stepp Revels

finding You easily

as You abide here
in my heart
with me always
bringing a song of peace
a dance of joy
a feeling
of comfort
finding
and knowing
You

~~~~~~~~~~~~~~~~~~

<u>Always and Forever</u>

When the pain comes
tearing at my heart
I feel

lost

down

alone
so alone

and my heart cries out
weeping from the feelings
my soul weary
as the emotions surround me
like sea waves threatening
I am drowning

Blessed

I hear Your voice
call my name
I feel You
reaching out to me
reassuring me
I am not alone

not alone

I move to You
tears streaming down my face
sobs causing my body to shake and tremble
as You reach out
draw me close to You
offering to me Your peace
the comfort of Your word, Your presence
in You
I find rest
in You

I find comfort
in You
with You

guiding me

along this journey
I have hope

my heart trembles
in the peace that is You
my soul sings
in the joy it finds

Rebecca Stepp Revels

in You

I stand once more
able to go on
feeling You
here
seeing You
in all things
hearing You
speak to me
I know
I know

I am not alone
You are my strength
my peace
in You
rests my faith

the tears dry
and my smile returns
for I know

when the pain comes
as it will
as long as I walk this journey

I do not walk it alone
for You dear Lord
are always and forever
with me.

Blessed

<u>Walking in Your Way</u>

Walking in Your way Lord
walking in Your light
how I want to go Lord
through this life
praising You
in everything
in the words I say
the songs
I sing
walking in Your way Lord
keeping my eyes to You
my every action
a reflection to You
my touch, one of compassion
whether gentle or strong
lifting up my brothers
as I travel along
walking in Your way Lord
as I travel this way
keeping my heart to You
and the coming day
walking in Your way Lord
with my heart to You
praying You're seen
in all that I do.

Rebecca Stepp Revels

<u>How I Stumble</u>

Lord how I stumble
falling easily at times
when temptation calls
words slip from my lips that shame me
how they must make you cry
hearing them
How I stumble
allowing emotions to control
actions that I do
turning my eyes from You
as I act, in earthly ways
not as a child of Yours
and the shame I feel, later
How I stumble
allowing myself to fall
when my heart cries no
this earthly places calls
and I slip off the narrow road
that leads to You
and I find myself crawling in the ditches
crying in my shame
How I stumble
how I cause you to weep
in my shame
I call to You in whispers
through my tears
and You hear
with tender compassion and understanding
with never ending mercy and grace
you reach out to me
and You bring me home
forgiving me once again
how I stumble

Blessed

Into the Grace

I stand in the shadow
feeling the pain
of a cruel, callus world
pushed aside and unwanted
as the cold seeps into my heart
tears slip and fall unnoticed
tracking cheeks already stained
by the tears shed before
hunger for something growls
as I tremble, here in the shadows
holding tightly to myself
holding on, to something unknown
seeking an answer,
to a question I haven't asked
seeking compassion, a way to peace
a way, from the shadows
into a different kind of sunlight
one I see, yet don't understand
then a voice calls my name
dries my tears, as I am wrapped securely
in a feeling of acceptance
compassion and loves flows around me
a peace never known before
envelopes me
as I step from the shadows of this world
a cold and lonely place
into the light
into the grace
into the love
of my Savior
the One, who called my name

Rebecca Stepp Revels

<u>So Blessed</u>

I am blessed Lord in You
I see that every day
in the morning sun, rising
bringing light to a darkened world
there is You, bringing light
to a darkened heart
a heart wounded and weary
that finds rest in You
I am blessed Lord, in You
as I see the crystal blue sky
the greens of the newly budding leaves
the flowers that emerge to dance in the breeze
I see You, even when the eyes are tired
of seeing the pain of this place
in You, in the gifts You give
I see a refuge, a shelter from the storm of this life
I know I am blessed
when I step out into this place
I find You waiting, wishing to walk with me
be with me in love as I find solace here
I hear Your voice, telling me
to be still and hear You
to be still and see You
to be still and know that You are Lord
I know I am blessed
as I feel You move in my heart
calming my storms, easing my fears
taking me to safe harbor in You to rest
when the tears flow freely
from a soul over joyed at Your presence
when the trembling comes as I feel You move
the smile spreads outward and my eyes look upward
to You, with raised hands I praise You
knowing I am so blessed

Blessed

when I see the compassionate acts of others
reaching out, as You inspire
when I hear a child sing and laugh
feel the touch of the aged, trembling and gentle
when I stand under the bows of a tree and watch a soft rain falling down
I know I am in the shelter of Your love
I know, Lord, I know
I am blessed.

~~~~~~~~~~~~~~~~~~~~~~~~~~~~~~~~

Along This Way

Along the paths of this world I walk
yet not alone
I feel Your presence
with me, walking by my side
I feel Your presence
in my heart, as my guide
I know You are with me
when I stumble and fall
lifting me up, strengthening me
to continue on
Traveling a journey that I must
doing all in my heart
with my hands
with my words
that I can to obey Your commands
to go and tell
to go and share
I try Lord

Rebecca Stepp Revels

with Your help in all things
to do as You would have me
in my weakness there are times I fail
but in coming to You, find strength and forgiveness
I rise up from my weakness
and walk on, feeling You here
knowing Your love
hoping, praying that as I walk
others will see You
seek You
come to know You
and in finding You,
find all of the mercies and love
that I have found
Walking with You Lord
I have found peace in the knowing
that along this way as I walk, I am not alone
In this peace, I find the desire
to share this love with others
in the hopes, that they will find You
along their own walk
through this place.

Blessed

You Are There

When the storm comes
You are there, standing strong
offering a shelter
from the winds and rain that fall
protection, from the suffering it brings
You are there,
offering strength, to lean on
when the storms grow stronger
when its elements, bring damage
You are there, offering comfort
after the storms pass away
a place of rest,
one filled with a peace
that can only come from you
When the storms come
You are there
as they fade away
and their winds cease
You are there
the rock to build on
the rock to stand on
You are there
in You, I am secure.

Rebecca Stepp Revels

<u>You Knew</u>

You knew
even before You came
You knew
what it was You would face
the things that awaited You
yet in Your great love
in the love of the Father You came
knowing
Walking among us
smiling, laughing, loving
teaching those that followed
healing the sick with a touch or a word
all the while, with each step
taking You closer
You knew
walking on water
calming a storm
calming the hearts
calming the spirits
of the weary
giving to them a place of rest
in You
bringing a special message
bringing to fact
the prophecies of old
by Your very being
as You walked the dusty, roads
sitting prayerfully in the garden
talking with the Father
You knew
when they came for You
at the appointed time

Blessed

You went, without hesitation
to Your death
hung on a cross
hung on a tree
the worst of deaths
painful and long
a crown of thorns shoved onto Your brow
as Your blood flowed down
the clouds gathered

the veil was rent
as You spoke
"It is finished"
You knew

when they came to the tomb
on the third day
and the angels waited
and sent them away
for You were not there
arisen
You had arisen
for a little more time
to walk among the believers
to show them, to show many
You were
as You said You would be
alive
as You knew
would happen
You knew
and You came
You knew
and You suffered
You knew

Rebecca Stepp Revels

and You died
You knew
now You live
You knew
and You love us still
forgiving us
all things
You knew, and You became the door
to eternity.

~~~~~~~~~~~~~~~~~~~~~~~~~~~~~

<u>He Lives</u>

He is risen
He is risen indeed
walking among us
alive, He's alive
death could not hold Him
death has lost
He is risen
living, waiting with the Father
for the time to come
He will return
He will come for His children
taking all into eternity with Him
defeating evil
bringing sweet peace
in Him, with Him
He is risen
He lives, He lives
and because He lives
we can receive forgiveness
because He lives
He offers us His merciful grace

Blessed

undeserved, unearned
given freely
the price is paid
was paid on the cross
in the time of the tomb
He is risen
He lives
because He lives
He has opened the doorway
the veil has been rent in two
He waits with open arms
waiting for me
waiting for you
offering life with Him
offering a gift, He hopes we will accept
He is risen
He is risen indeed
He lives
and He waits on us
with open arms.

Until That Day Comes

The day will come Lord
for one and for all
when You call us home
to finally walk with You
face to face
along the glorious streets of gold
until then,
I walk with You here
held deeply in my heart
knowing, You are with me
guiding me along
I walk for You
looking to others I pass

Rebecca Stepp Revels

wondering, if they know you as I do
do they walk with You, for You
or do they walk alone
The day will come
when You call my name from on High
and I know, this journey is done
I will walk from this life
into Your open arms
knowing true peace at last
joyous peace in Your presence
love in the radiance of Your smile
until then, I walk this journey
and I try, to be the child You would have me to be
walking in faith, walking in belief
knowing Your presence close
knowing Your love
offering, the semblance that I can
in a compassionate word
a gentle hand
hoping, in the walk, I show You
plant the seeds of love
that You would have me to plant
showing You, in the way that You are
not in the way I would have You to be
The day will come
when I hear You call to me
whispering, shouting, "Come home"
and with joyous shouts I will answer

running to You
as I leave this place behind
I run to You
never looking back

I run to You
hoping, that in some way

Blessed

in the wake of my passing
others will see You
others, will hear You
will come to You
walking with You in their heart
by their side, as their guide
walking, ready for the day
walking, doing all that they can
to show You, to share You
until the day comes
that You turn and call their name
bidding them, come home.

I Am At Peace

In You Lord,
I find great peace
unknown anywhere else
peace that brings me from the depths of despair
when the darkness closes in
threatening me once again
when it pulls at me
a voice from the darkness taunting
remember
I was there once, in that pit
mistakes I made
but I know Lord
in Your merciful grace
I am forgiven
You heard my cries
the moans of one lost in a darkness of their own making
trapped in misery
shackled by sin to this world
beaten and bruised
I was defeated and lost

Rebecca Stepp Revels

You reached into the mess where I cowered
pulling me from the darkness
bringing me back to You
bringing me to Your light and Your peace
wrapping me in Your love
granting me rest from the storms
a sanctuary from the battle of temptation
You are all Lord,
You are everything
In Your forgiveness
I am healed
In Your mercy
I am saved
In Your light,
I am whole
In Your Light
I am at peace

I Trust In You

I place my trust in You Lord
walking with You as I go
moving through this life
on my way, to eternity, with You
I hear You speaking to me
offering encouragement to me
when times are hard
and the storms come
You are here, with me
it is in You alone, I trust
to protect me, no matter how strong the wind blows
no matter how hard, the rain falls
You alone, are my shelter

Blessed

You alone, are the rock that I build upon
I trust in You
to be my light, when darkness threatens
guiding me away
guiding me to a calm port

I trust in You Lord
when worries come,
slipping in from the corners and cracks
waiting for me to pass
You take my hand, calm my fears
whisper, for me to listen
for You are here
always here
I feel Your presence,
I hear Your voice
as You call my name
I trust in You
and I know
peace.

~~~~~~~~~~~~~~~~~~~~~~~~~~~~~~

I Will Walk With You

into Your peace
I commend my spirit
into Your light
I offer my life
I want to walk with You
along this path
knowing, it is but a moment
into Your love
I walk, with arms open
holding tightly to what You offer
clinging, to what You give
knowing, it is forever
eternity waits, and You lead me there

Rebecca Stepp Revels

holding my hand
protecting my heart
as we travel
when the road grows hard
my body weak and weary
You carry me
when the trials come
You strengthen me
I trust in You
I offer my life, such as it is
to You
for You are my Lord
You are my King
You are my Savior
along this journey
I will walk with You
as You walk with me
I will hear Your voice
along this way
when it is at its darkest
I will place my faith in You
and we will dance.

Blessed

<u>Be Still</u>

When I listen Lord, to Your words
whispered into my heart
hear You telling me
'be still'
and I actually do
it is well,
I can understand
what it is You are telling me
and the storm will pass
much quieter
the winds die down
the rains fall more gently
as the clouds part with a whimper
when I stop, and listen to You
instead of acting on my own
for on my own, I act as the world does
and the storms only grow
out of my anger
because of my pain
as You call to me
'be still'
When my heart hears Your voice
my soul responds
as do the storms around me
hearing Your voice
and there is comforting peace
that comes to me
wrapping itself around me
assuring me, I am Your child
I am loved
when I hear Your voice
'be still'
I know, You are God.

Rebecca Stepp Revels

<u>He Is Risen</u>

Go and share
go and tell
let everyone know
the truth

He is risen
He is risen indeed

Death could not hold Him
the tomb no prison
He kept His word
as promised

He is risen
He is risen indeed

Waiting near
with arms open wide
knocking on the door
of our heart

He is risen
He is risen indeed

Calling to us
wanting us near
a relationship
with Him

He has risen
He has risen indeed

and He walks with us
loves us dearly

Blessed

look what He did
as He did

He is risen
He is risen indeed

and He asks
He instructs
He has given us what we need
to go and tell

He has risen
He has risen indeed.

and He is
coming back.
are you ready?

~~~~~~~~~~~~~~~~~~

Rebecca Stepp Revels

<u>In Your Awesome Wonder</u>

Standing here bathed in Your light
feeling Your love, wrapped around me
comforting me, bringing such peace
a calm in the midst of all storms
it is easy to forget
what lingers outside of Your light
it is easy to forget
where I was, once
lost and alone, reaching out for something
seeking, an escape from the pain
a way out, of the dark
when I heard Your voice
felt Your touch on my heart
calling me, drawing me
out of the shadows of despair
into Your glory and love
Standing here, feeling Your presence
as a friend, as a guide through the storm
I can become complacent, forget
You are Lord
Alpha and Omega, King of Kings
You are awesome, You are Mighty
To my knees Lord, I fall before You
trembling, not in fear
but in awestruck wonder
reminded, of Your power
reminded, of Your peace
I kneel here, humbly, willingly
face down Lord, knowing, remembering
who I am, and who it is, that You are
Your gentle touch of mercy
Your loving touch of grace
the forgiveness You readily give
forgetting our iniquity, the moment we give it to You

Blessed

turning away from it
to follow closely along with You
tears flow as Your love fills me
over flows from my heart into a thirsty spirit
as I remember where I was
as I understand, where I am
kneeling here, before You
wrapped, in Your awesome wonder
and Your glorious love.

Serenity and Song

An emotion I can not explain
a feeling that reaches in
wrapping around my heart
comfort and joy
peace and excitement
serenity and celebration
that is You Lord
and Your presence in my life
Feeling You move in my life
Your presence with me
letting me know
You are close
My soul knows You
feels You near to me,
and it sings praises to You
My soul feels You with me
and it dances
there is no other way, to explain
this feeling, moving in my heart
tears come to my eyes
a catch in my throat
an excitement, an electric feeling
that moves through me
and I feel, yes I feel

Rebecca Stepp Revels

that I can reach out,
and place my hand in Your wounds
I could reach out my hand
and grasp Your robe
and my ills would all be healed
my tears would all be dried
You are here, my heart feels You
my soul knows Your presence
and I can not help but smile
because of an emotion
difficult to explain
but impossible, not to feel
what reaches in
and touches my heart
alive, with serenity and song.

Your Light

When I feel, that this world has done me wrong
injured my heart, wounded my spirit
reaching out, trying to drag me down
into the pit, that I left behind, long ago
I turn to You, reaching out for You
and You hear me, calling out
crying in my desperation
trembling, in my pain
You see me, here on my knees
with hands raised to You
It is then, in the moments of my darkest hours
that I feel You the strongest
as I reach out to You,
I feel You, reaching out to me
comforting me in my sorrows, bringing to me Your peace
sweet and restful
You give to me, what I need, in the right time of my need
helping me to understand, the gifts that are from You
that moment of first sunlight, that brightens a long night

Blessed

those first drops of gentle rain, after the drought
the blessed feelings of Your presence, as the storms break around me
You are with me, always, making Your presence known in the small things
waiting for me, to open my eyes and see You here
waiting for me, to raise up weary arms, to feel You lift me up
waiting for me, to hear You speaking to me
reassuring me of Your presence, reassuring me of Your comfort
When it seems, that my world is at its darkest
that is when Your light, shines the brightest.

~~~~~~~~~~~~~~~~~~~~~~~~~~~~

Such Is

like gentle rain
falling down
so is Your comfort
a spring shower
softly falling
onto a thirsty earth
Your love
falling to quench
thirsty souls
sunlight warming the lands
waking it from winter's rest
Your peace
warming hearts cold and alone
with Your presence
a soft breeze
playing the leaves on the trees
such is Your love
feeding a hungry soul
giving it cause
to dance.

~~~~~~~~~~~~~~~~~~~~~~~~~~~~

Rebecca Stepp Revels

How Lord

How do I share Lord
the feeling that I have
when I feel You
so very close?
When the spirit within me moves
excited, that You are so near
when I want no matter where I am
to raise my arms to You
and praise Your name
as You make Your presence known
How do I share Lord
what do I say, that they will understand
how strong the joy is inside of me
knowing You, have set me free
forgiven me, of my wrongs
how You went to the cross, freely
how You could have saved Yourself
instead Lord, sweet Lord
You chose to save me
paying the price, no one else could pay
Tell me Lord, what to say
that they will hear
of how You rose again and You live
yes Lord, yes You live
and You wait, for all that will hear Your call
with Your arms open, Your heart ready
to receive all to You
how can I tell Lord
the feeling that I have
when I feel You moving
so very close
walking with me
guiding me always
to eternity, with You.

Blessed

<u>Into Your Peace</u>

Into Your peace I walk

surrendering my life

making it Yours

offering to You

all that I am

accepting from You

all that You offer to me

for I understand

it is Your great love

that surrounds me

comforts me in times of heartache

stress and fear

it is, Your love

that shows me a place of rest

when this body grows weary

Rebecca Stepp Revels

when fighting the battles of this walk

become too much to bear

all that I am, I give to You

use me Lord, as You will

I am a tool in Your hands

offered freely to You

in the hopes of planting a seed.

Sharing with those I meet

what You do for me

carrying Your light

into the darkness You have brought me from

into the darkness, I must pass through on this journey

Your love, keeps me strong as I go

Knowing, You are with me

I will fear nothing

as in Your presence, I walk.

Blessed

<u>A Gift of Boldness</u>

On this journey that I travel
through a land not my home
I ask You Lord
give to me a boldness
to speak of You
with those that I meet along the way
in a way, that they will listen
not in a way of arrogance
not in a way of judgment
but with a boldness
that shows of a knowledge of You
a true faith, in You
knowing, what You Lord, have done for me
in lifting me up from the pit I was in
in walking with me day to day
moment by moment
closer than anyone else could ever be
for I know, You are here with me,
Your Spirit residing in me
blessing me with the gift of Your love
giving to me, the words I need
giving to me, the compassion to care
and the knowledge between right and wrong
Lord, give to me a boldness
that as I go, I speak readily of You
for I know, time is short
Your return grows close
Those that have turned away, will be lost
those that have not heard, need the chance to know You
give me Lord, that desire
give to me Lord the way

to do as instructed, and go and tell
to share You
to share, how You have brought me so far
from where I was

Rebecca Stepp Revels

How I had wandered away, and yet You did not leave me alone
You stayed with me, protecting me
sheltering me, until I realized
until the day, I heard Your voice calling me back
calling me home
back into Your light
into Your mercy and grace unmeasured
Give to me Lord, I ask
a boldness to go out into this world
where there are so many that have not heard
a boldness to tell, to share You Lord
and Your love
For it is You, that has brought me so far
giving to me, another chance
back on the right path
back on that narrow road to You
the only way to Salvation
for You are the Door, the Way and the Light
only You
give to me Lord
the boldness I need
to go and tell
open the ears Lord, of those that hear
allow them to understand
open the eyes Lord
so that they may see
Time grows short Lord
give to me a boldness
to go and tell.

Blessed

<u>Hallelujah, Hosanna</u>

My heart sings out to You
my soul filled with joy
sings glory to Your name
for You are my King
my Savior
When I was lost
weary and afraid
You reached into the pit
and pulled me from the darkness
You brought me out
back into Your light
calming my fears
bringing me, to a place of rest
In You, I know joy
In You, I know pure love
In Your forgiveness,
I have found peace
uplifting, freeing peace
from the burdens that I have carried
You are my strength
my hope and my foundation
In You Lord
my heart sings
Hallelujah, Hosanna
glory to my King
In You Lord
my soul does shout
Hallelujah, Hosanna
glory to You my Lord
my all, my every thing.

Rebecca Stepp Revels

Words

Words whispered
from a worshipful heart

words sang
from a hopeful heart

words shouted
from joyous heart

words spoken
seeking the promise
speaking the faith
sharing the love

of a most holy and glorious Savior

words, meant to touch the heart
plant a seed
begin a relationship
or to make a relationship stronger

with Jesus Christ, Lord and Savior

Words of faith in the Light
when the darkness threatens all around.

Words from the heart
psalms of the soul
when the heart cannot help but sing
blessed, praise to the Son of the Most High
we are indeed blessed.

Blessed

www.ingramcontent.com/pod-product-compliance
Lightning Source LLC
Chambersburg PA
CBHW080244170426
43192CB00014BA/2561